Buddhist Education
in
Early Medieval India

Buddhist Education in Early Medieval India

Dr. Kameshwar Prasad

Kaveri Books
New Delhi-110 002

ISBN: 978-93-86463-13-5
First Published in 2021

Published by

Kaveri Books
4832/24, Ansari Road, Darya Ganj
New Delhi - 110 002 (India)

Tel.: 011- 4707 2321
E-mail: kaveribooks@gmail.com & info@kaveribooks.com
Website: www.kaveribooks.com

PRINTED IN INDIA

Dedicated to the sacred memory of

my wife

Madhavi Prasad

who could not see the publication of this book.

Preface

Indian contributions in the field of education has been of exceptional significance. It has left a rich heritage of education system for the posterity. Many educational centers flourished throughout India from ancient times onwards. Takshashila (Taxila) presently in Pakistan, was the earliest educational centre, renowned all over India, even before the emergence of the *Mahaviharas* as centres of higher Buddhist learning. In india two systems of education flourished side by side – the Brahamanical and the Buddhist or monastic. The former evolved around individual teachers and *gurukulas* or *acaryakulas*, temples, *mathas* and *agraharas*. With the spread of Buddhism several *Viharas* and *Mahaviharas* emerged as centres of Buddhist education throughout India in early medieval times, particularly in Bihar and Bengal. The most important of these were Nalanda, Odantapuri, Vikramshila, Jagaddal, Somapura and Vallabhi. Nalanda and Vikramshila acquired the status of international universities where students and scholars not only from every nook and corner of India but China, Tibet, Srilanka, Java, Sumatra, Nepal and other parts of globe congregated in large numbers in search of knowledge, particularly Buddhism. The fame and influence of these *Mahaviharas* was not confined to Bihar and Bengal only but spread all over India. The Chinese and the Tibetan accounts describe splendours as well as working of these *Mahaviharas.* Inscriptions, seals and architectural remains discovered during excavations of the sites of these *Mahaviharas* further enrich our knowledge about these Buddhist educational centres. Recently existence of two more *Mahaviharas* in Bihar have come to light as a result of excavations. These are (i) *Sri Prathamashipur Mahavihara* (Telhara) and (ii) *Srimaddharmavihara* (Lakhisarai).

The present study deals mainly with the Buddhist system of education in early medieval India but focus is on Bihar as it was here that the main *Mahaviharas* thrived and went into oblivion. The study is based mainly on the Chinese and Tibetan literary accounts. Exavation reports of the relevant sites have also been fully utilised. Available photographs from excavated sites have been provided to make the study more meaningful and interesting.

I take this opportunity to express my sense of gratitude to all those scholars who have worked earlier on the subject and whose works have been utlised in this book. Many friends and scholars helped me in different ways in the completion of this work. My sincere thanks are due to them. Dr. Chitta Ranjan Prasad Sinha, former Director, K. P. Jayaswal Research Institute, Patna, Dr. Umesh Chandra Dwivedi, former Director, Museums, Government of Bihar, Patna and Dr. (Ms) Kiran Kumari, Associate Professor, Department of Sanskrit, Ganga Devi Mahila College, Patliputra University, Patna, deserve my special thanks who helped considerably in the completion of this book. I am also thankful to Dr. Akal Ram, my former Research Scholar and presently Post-Doctoral Fellow, Department of History, Patna University who took over himself the burden of getting typed the manuscript and procuring books from libraries for me. Last, but not the least, I express my sincere gratitude to Shri Rakesh Goel of Kaveri Books, New Delhi, for publishing this book in short time and with attractive getup. Thanks to all of them.

Kameshwar Prasad

Patna
Basant Panchami
16 February 2021

Contents

List of Plates

Introduction

India is renowned for its achievements not only in political, socio-economic, religious, artistic and literary spheres but intellectual field as well. It evolved from very early times a sound system of education which developed and matured gradually. It was an unique system of education which began at home and gradually developed in *gurukulas, mathas,* temples, *agraharas, Viharas* and *Mahaviharas*. Many such educational centres emerged from ancient times. Takshashila and Mithila became chief centres of Vedic religious teaching. The *Viharas* and *Mahaviharas* imparted teaching of Buddhist theology. Thus, two parallel systems of education evolved in India – The Brahamanical and the Buddhist or monastic. Utmost importance was laid on the education of a man. A man devoid of education was considered as incompetent to discharge his social duties. The basic aim of education was to develop physical, moral, religious and social responsibilities. It also aimed at preserving and spreading elements of national heritage and culture.

The Brahamanical or Vedic system was the earliest form of education in India. In this system family and *gurukulas* run by renowned scholar sages played significant role. The education of the child began with some rituals, the most important being the *Upanayan* ceremony. After performance of this ceremony which was long and clumsy, the student became a *brahmacari*. Strict rules were made for him which could not be violated. The *brahmacari* was sent to the *gurukula* where he studied for a fixed time. Having completed his studies the student entered the *grihastha ashram*. Education in the *gurukulas* was free. These educational institutions were financially run on the basis of *gurudakshina* and donations from kings, pious, rich and liberal people. Apart from *gurukulas*, there were brahmana *mahasalas* akin to Vedic schools. There were many such schools in Magadha-Anga region during the time of king Bimbisara of Magadha. Several hermitages also imparted education. During early medieval times Mithila became the main centre of brahamanical studies, particularly in the field of *Nyaya* and *Mimamsa*. The brahamanical system of education existed at least upto early medieval times, despite emergence of monastic system in north india. The brahamanical tradition was carried on by temples and *agraharas* in South India.

The emergence of Buddhism in 6th century BCE brought about significant transformation in social and religious life. In the time of Gautam Buddha and even after his *Mahaparinirvana*, Buddhism spread rapidly in the then Magadha region. This was because of the missionary zeal of the Buddhist monks during the life time of Buddha and even after him. Buddhist *Viharas* or monasteries were set up at several places for the residence of monks. These monasteries soon turned as centres or schools for the teaching of Buddhist religion and philosophy. The Kutagarasala at Kolhua in Vaishali, where Buddha mostly resided and sermoned, became one of the main centres of Buddhist teaching. In subsequent times many of these *Viharas* turned into *Mahaviharas* or centres of higher studies comparable to universities. These were located mostly in the then Bihar and Bengal. Buddhist monasteries could not develop in South India due to weak Buddhist influence and strong Vaishnavite and Shaivite hold there during early medieval times. The brahamanical and the monastic system of education, which ran side by side, had some common features but the differences are more prominent. The basic difference between the two was that the brahamanical system prepared the student to enter the second *ashram* of life but the monastic system did not expect students to return to family life. Rather the students were expected to renounce the family life and devote themselves to the propogation of tenents of Buddhism.

The literary–mainly Chinese and Tibetan and archaeological sources attest the existence of several *Viharas* and *Mahaviharas* in Bihar and Bengal. Noteworthy amongst them are the Mahabodhi *Samgharama*, Vajrasana Mahabodhi monastery, Jivakarama *Vihara*, Yasovarmapura *Vihara*, Prathamashipur *Vihara*, Svastika *Vihara*, Srimaddharma *Vihara*, Kukutapadigiri *Vihara* also known as Apanaka *Mahavihara*, the *Mahaviharas* of Nalanda, Odantapuri, Vikramshila, Jagaddal, Somapura and Vallabhi in Gujrat. The Chinese accounts refer to several monasteries situated in Uttar Pradesh, the most important being the Jetvana *Vihar* in Sravasti. The remains of Pushpagiri *Vihara* and Madhapura *Mahavihara* have come to light from Odisha. The former flourished between 3rd and 11th centuries and the latter between 7th and 12th centuries CE. Excavations of several of these sites have exposed structural remains of monasteries, seals, sealings and inscriptions which enlighten us on the history of these *Viharas* and *Mahaviharas*. The most important of these *Mahaviharas* were Nalanda, Odantapuri and Vikramshila. We have, therefore, concentrated our attention on them. As both Somapura and Jagaddal (Jogoddol) *Mahaviharas* are presently located in Bangladesh, they have been left out of consideration.

Of all the *Mahaviharas* Nalanda, identified with village Badgaon and group of villages, is the most important. The site has been continuously explored and excavated since the first visit of the site by Francis Buchanan in 1811-12. Later on Kittoe, Cunningham, Marshall, Broadley, Spooner and others made small and large excavations at the site. Birendra Nath excavated the site of Sarai Mound. These excavations have yielded rich archaeological material in the form of structural remains, seals and sealings, inscriptions and other antiquarian remains. Hsuan Tsang, I-Tsing and Dharmasvamin give detailed account of Nalanda. The history of Nalanda suggests that it was a religious place from the very beginning and was visited both by Vardhaman Mahavira and Gautam Buddha. It was the birth place of Sariputra. Therefore, Mauryan king Ashoka got constructed here for the first time a *Vihara*. Later on Sakaraditya or Kumargupta I of the Gupta dynasty built here a *Samgharma* in 5th century of the Christian era. Since then prosperity of Nalanda grew unabated. Later Gupta kings, Maukharis, Harshavardhan, Yasovarman and Pala kings of Bengal and Bihar added many *Viaharas* and *Chaityas*. By the first half of the 8th century CE Nalanda had fully developed in a monastic establishment. As many as 11 monasteries and several Temples (*Chaityas*) were exposed during excavations. Temple no. 3 is very imposing and the highest monument. Temple no. 2 contained the dado of 211 sculptured panels over the moulded plinth. Sarai Mound temple exposed a polychrome painting all around *garbhagriha* hall. Besides, remains of many *stupas* and monastic cells for monks were also brought to light during excavations. Towards the close of the 12th century CE Nalanda suffered badly due to Turkish raids.

The fame of Nalanda rests on being the seat of higher Buddhist studies. Students and scholars from different parts of India as well as abroad came in large numbers in search of knowledge. The *Mahavihara* had nearly 4000 students and 1500 teachers. There was a galaxy of teachers (*Pandits*). Some of these were Dinnaga, Asanga, Vasuvandhu, Sthirmati, Silabhadra, Santideva, Buddhakirti and Dipankarasrijnan Atisa. The *Mahavihara* had made rules for admission to the monastery. The admission seeker was to pass the oral entrance test taken by the *Dwarapandits*. There were four *Dwarapandits* at four gates of the *Mahavihara*. They were themselves renowned scholars. Free boarding and lodging was provided to the students. The students had to follow a fixed time-table and strictly observe rules of discipline. Nalanda had developed its own curriculum which included not only theology, but language, logic, philosophy, *tantra*, medicine, science and other subjects. The teaching was oral and through debates and discussions. Copying of manuscripts was regularly done. Stress was put on the teaching of *Mahayana*. The relation between teachers and students was very cordial. We do not come across any instance of student unrest. The *Mahavihara* had very rich library

(*Dharmaganj*) where original and copied manuscripts were kept. It had three sections – Ratnasagar, Ratnodadhi and Ratnakaranda.

A sound system of management of the *Mahavihara* was also developed. It was run by scholars and monks themselves residing there. The monastery enjoyed full autonomy. It had its own seal. The *Sthavira* was the highest priest. *Paripalaka* or abbot seems to be main administrator. Besides, there were other functionaries choosen on the basis of merit. There was also a management committee to look after the affairs of the monastery. The expenses of the monastery were met by support from the kings as well as villages. According to I-Tsing 200 villages were attached to the *Mahavihara* to supply essentials to the monastery. The Pala king Devapala granted five villages to the monastery built by Balaputradeva, king of Suvarnadvipa. Some *agraharas* and *Viharas* were also attached to Nalanda *Mahavihara*. Hsuan Tsang and I-Tsing were two distinguished Chinese scholars and the Tibetan monk Dharmasvamin who resided for some times at Nalanda. They have left valuable account of Nalanda *Mahavihara*.

Odantapuri *Mahavihara* was established in Pala period near Nalanda at Biharsharif. Its exact location in Biharsharif is uncertain as extensive excavation could not be conducted due to abundance of medieval buildings and tombs in old Biharsharif town. It was probably situated at Bari Pahadi. The credit for establishing Odantapuri *Mahavihara* is given to the Pala king Gopala (750-780 CE). It was on the model of Odantapuri *Mahavihara* that Santarakshita built Samye *vihara* in Tibet. Odantapuri flourished under the rule of the Pala kings. Details about this *Mahavihara* is scanty. The Tibetan accounts throw some light on this educational centre. Taranatha suggests that 1000 monks lived at Odantapuri permanently. *Mahayana* Buddhism with its special feature of *Tantrayana* seems to be the chief subject of study. Compared to Nalanda it was a smaller monastery but famous as centre of *Tantric* studies. The most important contribution of Odantapuri was that it developed its own alphabet known as *Bhaikshuki.* Tibetan, than the Chinese influence was more prominent at Odantapuri.

The system of education at Odantapuri was similar to Nalanda. Education was imparted orally, sometimes through lectures. However, there were no entrance tests. Writing was also done here. Several texts were prepared here. The copying of manuscripts was also done on large scale. The monastery thrived on the financial support of Pala kings, local feudatories and local people. Odantapuri had a number of scholars, the most important of them being Santarakshita and Dipankarasrijnan Atisa. Out of the traditional 84 *Siddhas,* Yoga-pa and Santi-pa were also associated with Odantapuri *Mahavihara.* Towards the end of the 12th century CE Odantapuri was also destroyed by the Turks. The destruction was so complete that no remains of it exists.

Vikramshila *Mahavihara* was yet another centre of higher Buddhist studies. It was famous for *Tantric* studies. Great controversy prevailed for long time regarding its exact location. The archaeological excavations conducted at village Antichak near Kahalgaon by the Department of Ancient Indian History and Archaeology, Patna University and the Archaeological Survey of India finally settled the problem of the identification and location of the site in favour of Antichak. This *Mahavihara* was got constructed by the Pala king Dharmapala in 8th century CE. The excavations exposed the entire plan of the monastic complex, central shrine, 253 monastic cells and other architectural remains including library. The most important inscription discovered from here was that of Sahura, a local ruler. Some seals and sealings were also discovered from the site. Lama Taranatha gives some information about this *Mahavihara.* Vikramshila had close links with Tibet and Nepal unlike Nalanda which was connected with China.

Like Nalanda, Vikramshila was an educational institution of international repute. It developed a sound system of education. Admission to the monastery was made on the basis of oral enterance test like Nalanda. However, where Nalanda had only four *Dwarapandits* to conduct the test, there were six *Dwarapandits* in Vikramshila. A student seeking admission in the *Mahavihara* had to satisfy these *Dwarapandits* who were eminent scholars. Main stress was put on the teaching of *Tanrayana* and *Vajrayana,* though teaching of other subjects, specially logic, was not neglected. Stress was also put on copying of manuscripts. Tutorial system, debates and discussions were special features of the teaching methodology. Vikramshila had a rich library which had valuable collection of manuscripts, specially on *Tantra*. Rules of discipline were enforced strictly. Free lodging and boarding was provided to students and scholars residing there. Vikramshila did not enjoy autonomy like Nalanda. The reigining Pala kings exercised considerable influence over its affairs. On the completion of studies degrees or diplomas of *Pandit* were conferred on scholars. Something like convocation was held wherein the ruling Pala king conferred degrees on scholars.

Vikramshila *Mahavihara* had a galaxy of eminent scholars and surpassed Nalanda in this respect. Lama Taranatha informs us about twelve *Tantric acaryas* and six *Dwarapandits* of Vikramshila. Besides, many *Siddhas* were also connected with Vikramshila *Mahavihara*. The entrance wall of the *Mahavihara* was decorated with the portraits of eminent *acaryas*. Some of the eminent scholars of Vikramshila were Buddhajanapada, Ratnakarsanti, Vagishwarkirti, Naropa, Dipankarasrijana Atisa, Jetari, Abhyankargupta and Sakyasribhadra. From the time of Sakyasribhadra the political situation deteriorated due to Turkish raids. Therefore, many monks left Vikramshila, went to Tibet and settled there. Thus, by end of the 12th century CE like other *Mahaviharas* Vikramshila also went into oblivion.

The decline and desertion of the *Mahaviharas* of early medieval India poses many serious questions. The most important of these is how and why the *Mahaviharas* lost their eminence and existence. The Tibetan accounts of Lama Taranatha and Dharmasvamin hint at some of the causes of the decline of these monasteries. These were political anarchy and

Turkish raids. Both the factors are historically proven, but these were not the only causes for the decline of the *Mahaviharas*. We have to look elsewhere to satisfactorily explain the decline of the monasteries. In this context several religious and socio-economic causes may be analysed. Secterian conflicts and inherent vices in *Tantrayana, Mantrayana, Vajrayana* and *Sahajayana* contributed largely in decline. *Tantricism* adopted such rituals which was not acceptable to common people. Use of wine and women in monasteries polluted the atmosphere of monasteries and had devastating impact on common people. As a reaction monks and monasteries lost the sympathy and support of the masses. The social inequality, caste rigidity, untouchability also prevented support to the monasteries. In the atmosphere of political instability economic support to the monasteries collapsed. The final onslaught made by the Turks completely destroyed the *Mahaviharas*. They could not re-emerge either under the Sultans of Delhi, The Mughals, The East India Company or the British Crown.

1

An Outline of the Brahamanical Education

India's fame rests not only on empire building, ushering in an age of new religious ideas and philosophy but also due to its stress on intellectual activities. It evolved a system of education that continued and strengthened in coming centuries. Here, we notice two distinct systems of education imparted by the Brahamanical hermitages and Buddhist *Viharas*. *Rsis* and brahamanas spread Vedic religion and culture through their *gurukula* system while the Buddhist *Viharas* became centres of Buddhist learning marked by tennets of Buddhist religion and philosophy. Comparatively speaking the *gurukula* system could not become widespread with its inherent shortcomings but the monastic education became more and more widespread and popular. No *gurukula* could evolve in large centre of education but several monasteries developed into renowned centres of education and acquired the status of 'university' or *Mahavihara* where scholars and knowledge seekers flocked not only from different parts of India but foreign land as well. We find reference to several such educational centres in contemporary literary accounts, more particularly in the Chinese and Tibetan sources. Archaeological evidences in the form of seals, inscriptions, structures and sculptures discovered from famous *Mahavihara* sites also enlighten us on the subject. Thus, apart from Mithila, being the chief centre of Vedic religion and teaching, we also come to know about several monasteries (*Viharas*) which became chief centres of Buddhist education in

Bihar. To name a few of them, mention may be made of Pataliputra, Vajrasana (Bodh Gaya), Nalanda, Odantapuri, Vikramshila, Teladhaka, Dharawat, Ghosrawan and Fullhari. Of these Nalanda, Odantapuri and Vikramshila developed into *Mahaviharas* and became the chief centres of education. Neither Takshashila, Vallabhi, or even Jagaddala or Somapura could compete with the fame and glory of Nalanda and Vikramshila. However, the Jains could not contribute much to the growth of education, though Jain monks did not lag behind in scholarship and producing vast mass of literature. Jain temples did not develop into public centres of higher education.[1]

THE BRAHAMANICAL SYSTEM OF EDUCATION

In India both brahamanical and monastic systems of education flourished. Brahamanical or Vedic system of education was older than the monastic system. Its origin can be traced back to the Rg.Vedic times. It gradually developed and continued at least upto the medieval times. Even after the establishment of regular schools and centres of higher education in medieval and modern times, the brahamanical system continued in some form in temples, *mathas* and *agraharas*, specially in South India. The Vedic system of education initially began with the family itself. Family occupied the most important place in the scheme of education of children. The child learnt the first lesson about his culture and tradition or even profession from his father, mother or other elderly persons of the family. The ancient Indians assumed that the child began to receive influences that moulded his character and efficiency even before his birth, i.e., right from the time of conception. It was believed that the impressions, which would be conveyed on the mind of the expectant mother, would be automatically transmitted to the mind of the child to be born. The mother, therefore, was advised to devote herself to the study and contemplation of the achievements and biographies of great national heroes and heroines, so that she may herself get a child that may be a worthy successor of theirs.[2] Here we are reminded of the story of Abhimanyu, son of Arjuna given in the *Mahabharata*, who learnt the art of coming out of *chakravyuha* while still in his mother's womb. After his birth the child received primary education in the family itself. Later on the child received education in the *gurukulas* or *acaryakulas* under the patronage of renowned *risis* who also worked as teachers. Different stages are marked in the evolution of brahamanical education. These are;

(i) Vedic period,

(ii) Post-Vedic or the age of the *Upanishadas*, the *Sutras* and the *Epics*,

(iii) the age of the *Dharmasastras*, and

(iv) the age of the *Puranas* and *Nibandhas*.[3]

Thus, it can be viusalised that the brahamanical system of education originated in the Vedic period itself with the advent of the Aryans and fully developed by early medieval times.

AIMS AND IDEALS OF EDUCATION

A pertinent question which arises here is about aims and ideals of education in ancient India. Was it designed to prepare students for state services, or earn their livelihood or preserve and spread knowledge and culture through them? The literary texts of the period speak of high ideals of education. Education was regarded as a source of illumination. It is said that "education nourishes us like the mother, directs us to the proper path like the father, and gives us delight and comfort like the wife. It increases our fame, destroys our difficulties and makes us purer and more cultured. When we are in the solitude of a journey, or of a foreign country, it serves us as a valued companion. It is thus, a veritable desire-yielding tree."[4] A person devoid of education may be described as blind and incompetent to fulfill his obligations to himself as well as the society. Ancient Indian education was regarded not merely as book learning but overall development–physical, intellectual as well as moral–of the student.

The basic aims and ideals of ancient Indian education were to infuse a spirit of piety and religiousness, development of personality, inculation of civic and social duties, promotion of social efficiency and preservation and spread of national culture.[5] As religion played a dominant role in the life of the early Aryans and the teachers were normally *risis* and priests, much stress was put on the infusion of a spirit of piety and religiousness in the mind of the student. This was achieved through regular performance and observations of rituals and *vratas*. It fostered a spirit of piety and religiousness in the mind of the young pupil and enabled him to withstand the temptations of the worldly life. However, it did not expect the student after completion of education to renounce the world like Buddhists and Jains, rather expected him to become a pious and useful member of the society. The formation of character by the proper development of moral teaching by teachers helped considerably in character formation. Similarly, much stress was put on the development of personality by eulogising the feeling of self-respect, encouraging the sense of self-confidence, inculcating the virtue of self-restraint and by fostering the power of discrimination and judgement. Self-confidence was fostered through the *Upanayana* ceremony. The element of self-restrain further enriched the personality of pupil. Self-discipline was promoted by following proper habits taught by the teacher during the course of education. Stress was put on the performance of civic and social duties also. The student was expected not to lead a self-centred life but to transmit the acquired knowledge to others. Promotion of social efficiency and happiness was another aim of ancient Indian education. It was sought to be realised by proper training of the new generation in different branches of knowledge, professions and industries. By doing so the educational system contributed significantly to the general progress and happiness of the society. The most important aim of ancient Indian education was to preserve as well as spread elements of national heritage and culture. The theory of three debts–to gods, *risis* and ancestors–helped considerably the student to discharge his obligations properly in preserving and spreading national heritage and culture. Thus, the aim of ancient Indian education was to develop physical, mental, intellectual and spiritual capability of students.

EDUCATIONAL RITUALS

A significant feature of ancient Indian education system was the performance of some rituals at the beginning of the education of the child. Three such rituals are mentioned in the brahamanical literature. These were *Vidyarambha (Aksharas-vikaranam)*, *Cudakarana* and *Upanayana*. The *Vidyarambha sanskara* was performed at the commencement of the primary education of the child. It was to be performed at the time when the child became five years old. It was very much similar to the *Bismillakhani* ceremony prevalent among the Muslims at the beginning of the primary education.[6] The *Vidyarambha* ceremony was a simple one. It was performed on an auspicious day on which the child was to learn the alphabets for the first time. This ceremony could be performed by children of all castes.[7] The student was asked to worship Hari, Lakshami, Vinayaka and Saraswati, the goddess of learning. Besides, the child was also to follow ancestral worship *(sva-vidya)*, the *Sutrakaras* of that *vidya* and the *vidya* or subject of his choice. The worship of the deities was followed by that of the primary teacher and the child was then handed over to him. The teacher used to make the pupil write on rice all the alphabets with the help of a specially prepared golden or silver pen.[8] Suitable presents and offerings to the teacher and other brahamanas invited on the occasion marked the termination of the ceremony. The students studying before *Upanayana* were known as *Dandamanavakas*.[9] However, it may be pointed out here that this *sanskara* does not find mention in the *Grihyasutra* or *Dharamasutra* literature but only in late works belonging to early centuries of the Christian era, perhaps due to the fact that the art of writing had not developed by that time. This argument does not seem to be sound as the art of writing had definitely emerged by the 3rd century BCE (leaving apart the Harappan script). The probable reason for prescribing *Vidyarambha sanskara*, has been suggested by Altekar. He argues that in course of time the Vedic Sanskrit ceased to be the spoken language, the sciences of exegesis and grammar were developed and the art of writing was invented or borrowed. Even the memorising of the Vedic hymns required some previous elementary education. *Upanayan* could, therefore, no longer mark the beginning of education and a different ritual called *Vidyarambha* began to be recommended for the commencement of primary education."[10]

The *Vidyarambha* ceremony was followed by *Cudakarana* or tonsure and *Upanayana* ceremony. Perhaps for long time both *Vidyarambha* and *Cudakarna* were combined together. The *Arthasastra* of Kautilya (1.2.) clearly hints at it regarding the education of the prince. It says that the *Vidyarambha* for a Prince who was duly tonsured meant that he was to learn writing and numbers (वृतचौलकर्मा लिपि संख्यानं चोपयुज्जीत).

THE *UPANAYANA* CEREMONY

The formal and regular introduction of the student (*brahamacari*) began with the *Upanayana* ceremony. The term *Upanayana* consists of two words *upa* and *ni*, and literally means the introduction of the pupil. This introduction is not to the teacher by his father rather the teacher introduces the student to *brahamacarya*, the first stage of the *ashrama* system. The English rendering of the term *Upanayana* is given as 'Thread ceremony', which, however, does not convey its real meaning and significance. It may be pointed out that even in modern times many *savarna* and rich families perform *Yajnopavita* ceremony akin to the *Upanayana* ceremony. However, the *Upanayana* was much more significant. A late text *Viramitrodaya* describes *Upanayana* as the ceremony by which a *dvija* (twice born) is brought into contact with the following, viz., *Guru, Vrata, Veda, Yama, Niyama* and the *Devtas*.[11] It was a long ceremony and full of rituals. The Vedic literature, more particularly the *Dharmasutras* describe in detail this ceremony and analyse the significance of every ritual.

The law givers prescribe *Upanayana* mainly for the brahamanas, kshatriyas and vaisyas. The sudras were not entitled to perform this ceremony. However, Baudhayana allows the sudras also to perform the *Upanayana* ceremony. He remarks, "Let him initiate a Brahamana in spring, a Kshatriya in summer, a Vaisya in autumn, a Rathakara in the rainy season; or all of them in spring" (*Baudhayana Grhaya Sutra*, ii, 5, 8-9). Although three upper *varnas* were allowed *Upanayana* but *varna* considerations influenced the age and time of *Upanayana* as well as dress and rituals performed by the *brahamacari*. The age of *Upanayana* varied from 8 to 12 years. It also varied with particular aim (*Apastamba*, i, 1,1, 21-26). Like age, the time (season) of *Upnayana* also varied *varna*-wise. The ceremony opened with a breakfast, followed by shave and bath. The outer outlook of the child was changed. He was asked to wear *ajina* (upper garment), *vasa* (lower garment) and *mekhala* (girdle) and *yajnopavita*. He was also given a *danda* or staff of wood. All these equippages had special spiritual connotations. The rules for dressing hair were also prescribed. Having been dressed properly the pupil was presented before the teacher who made preliminary enquiries before admitting him to the *brahamcarya*. Prayaers to different deities were offered before the *asmarohana* ceremony (to stand on a stone as a symbol of steadfastness at study). It was only after the performance of these rituals that the teacher finally accepted the boy as his student. On this occasion the teacher commanded, "A Brahamacharin art Thou! Drink water. Do the service. Do not sleep in the day-time. Devoted to the teacher, study the Veda" (*Asvalyana Grhaya Sutra* i, 22, 2). Some other authorities also suggest the duty of 'putting of fuel'. Now the pupil was ready to move on the path of *brahmcarya* (literally meaning attendance on *Brahma* or *Veda*). The actual initiation began with the recitation of the *Savitri mantra*, more popularly known as the *Gaytri mantra*. By this *mantra* prayer is offered to god Sun to endow the *brahmacari* health, wealth and intellect.[12] For three days after the *Upanayana* the student was believed to remain in an embryonic condition, it was on the fourth day that his spiritual birth (second birth) took place. The preceptor or the teacher now performed the *medhajanana* rite wherein gods were invoked to develop *brahamacari's* mental powers. Henceforth the *brahmacarya* or studentship formally begins in teacher's house.

The law books prescribe strict rules and regulations which

the *brahamcari* had to follow. His food, daily works, service to the teacher, rules of study were all prescribed and were to be followed by the pupil. The teacher, on his part, was to take care of the student and treat him as his own son. Such high ideals are not to be found anywhere else in the world, not even in the monastic system of education in ancient India. The *samavartana* ritual marked the end of the period of *brahamcarya* and his education and he could return to his family by offering *gurudakshina* to his teacher.[13] Apart from *Upanayana* for Vedic education, literary texts also suggest that separate system of *Upanayana* was in practice for Ayurvedic and Dhanurvedic studies. Both Charaka and Susruta, *ayurvedacaryas* of ancient India provide for a special *Upanayana* ceremony for students seeking admission to medical studies. Similarly, provision of special *Upanayana* was made for the study of military science.[14]

DIFFERENT STAGES OF BRAHAMANICAL EDUCATION

The brahamancial system of education began with the *Vedas* itself. The *Rg.Veda* (X.109.4) suggests two stages and types of educational method. The matter of the hymns of the *Rg.Veda* are the direct outcome of the first method, i.e; realisation of the highest truth and its direct contemplation *tapas* which marks out the *risi* or "seer". The *Rg.Veda* refers to seven *risis*, absorbed in *tapas (tapasya)*. Then there were *munis* also. They were composers of the Vedic hymns and it was through them that the Vedic knowledge spread. In fact every *risi* became a teacher who imparted his son the text of knowledge which he had himself acquired. His hermitage functioned as a Vedic school. He admitted young students and instructed them in the literature or texts in his possession. The students were to understand and recite the text orally. In the *Rg.Veda* we get glimpses of the educational system which comprised of small domestic schools with resident pupils who followed prescribed discipline or vows and were known as *vratacaris*. This form later on developed in the *Gurukula* system and the student came to be known as *brahmacari* after performing the *Upanayana*. The successful students then moved to the Brahamana *Samghas*, the Assemblies or Academics for advancement of knowledge by discussing their respective contributions to it. Thus, "the conference method for the promotion and diffusion of learning, the method of discussion in seminars and academics was first evolved in India, as evidenced by the *Rg.Veda*."[15]

It is interesting to note that though the seers and *risis* generally belonged to brahamana *varna* but there are also instances of kshatriya *risis* (Ambarisha, Trasdasyu etc., *Rg.Veda* I, 100, 17). Similarly we have also reference to women *risis* known as *Risikas* and *Brahamavadinis* like Lopamudra (*Rg.Veda*, I, 179, 1-6), Apala (*Ibid.*, viii, 91, 1-7), and several others. By the later Vedic period the brahamanical system of education further evolved. The *Atharvaveda* (xi, 5) contains a long hymn describing the system of studentship. The organisation and machinery for the preservation and propagation of Vedic literature based on oral tradition developed in different types of institutions like *Sakhas, Charanas, Parishads, Kulas, Gotra* etc. The Vedic literature also informs us about the period of studentship, duties of students, the discipline to be followed, duties of teachers, relation between the teacher and the student, method of study and other allied subjects. The subject of study included besides the *Vedas* several other *vidyas* like *Itihasa-Purana, gatha, vyakhyana, akhyana, nakshatra-vidya, sutra, Upanishad, Brahma-vidya* etc. Some famous teachers of the time are also mentioned including king Janaka of Mithila whose court was the centre of Vedic religion and culture.[16] Both Yajnavalkaya and his wife Maitreyi were associated with the court of Janaka and participated in many disputations. By this time three distinct brahamanical educational institutions—homes of teachers as schools, debating circles and *parishadas* (academics) and conferences had emerged. In Bihar Videha (Mithila) emerged as the chief centre of brahamanical learning.

THE GURUKULA SYSTEM

An important feature of the brahamanical system of education was the institution of *Gurukula* or *acaryakula*. It was regarded as one of the pillars of *dharma* (*Taittiriya Upanishad,*

1.4). In this system a student after his *Upanayana,* went and stayed till the completion of his education in the house of his *guru* or preceptor. Such students were known as *antevasin* or *acaryakula-vasi.* They had to live under the patronage and guidance of the teachers, follow strict rules of discipline and devote their time and energy in studies as well as service of the teacher. The long and continued association of pupil with his teacher enabled him to emulate the example of his teacher who were renowned scholars. The system eliminated the factors in home life prejudicial to the educational atmosphere and facilitated better studies. Such *gurukulas* were normally set up in localities either in forests or away from the din of the city life. The students were provided free boarding and lodging in the *gurukulas.* It was only after the completion of their studies or the prescribed period of their stay in the *gurukula* that they offered *gurudakshina* to their teachers according to their resources and capabilities. The affairs of the *gurukula* were managed by the *acarya* himself with the help of senior students or *agrashisyas.* The *gurukulas* were run on the financial support provided by their own wealth in the form of land, orchards, cattle, begging by the students, *gurudakshina* and also gifts provided by the former students. Pious and rich sections of the society as well as kings also might have helped economically to run these unique educational institutions.

The brahamanical system of education continued to flourish at least upto the early medieval times, despite the emergence of monastic system of education. Apart from Mithila, Anga and Magadha also emerged as centres of brahamanical studies. Mithila or Videha was, of course, the chief centre of brahamanical education. It was just like a University, but not a University in the strict sense of the term as there was no centralised system of education or admission of the pupils. It may be termed as a University only in the sense that it was a renowned centre of advanced learning where many outstanding scholars lived and taught different subjects.[17] King Janaka of Mithila himself was a renowned scholar and took keen interest in scholarly disputations. He maintained close contact with

Kuru-Pancala, another famous seat of brahamanical studies. Scholars like Yajnavalkya, his wife Gargi, Uddalaka, Jabala and many others assembled in the court of Janaka. Scholars from other parts of the country also came there in search of knowledge. The spread of education also led to the growth of a vast literature on different subjects.

The early Buddhist texts attest the existence of brahamanical system of education in different parts of ancient Bihar. They refer to brahamana *mahasalas*, akin to Vedic schools, where three hundred to five hundred students studied and were financially supported by kings. Several such institutions existed in the Anga-Magadha region in the time of king Bimbisara of Magadha. We learn from the *Mahagovinda Suttanta* (*Digha Nikaya*, 1.114) that Mahagovinda established seven *mahasalas* in seven main kingdoms of his time, one of which was Anga with its capital at Champa. It is also said that each of the *mahasala* had not less than three hundred brahamana students. Apparently these were superior to Vedic schools and may be termed as 'brahamanic colleges', exclusively for the brahamanas. Besides, there were several hermitages in Vaishali, Rajagriha and Bodh Gaya where renowned teachers imparted education. The *Majjhima Nikaya* informs us that two famous teachers Alara Kalama and Rudraka Ramaputra lived between Rajagriha and Uruvela (Bodh Gaya) and taught the students. Gautam Buddha is said to have visited Alara Kalama at Vaishali before going to Uruvela. Besides, the *parivrajakas* constituted a travelling school. Later on Pataliputra also emerged as a centre of brahamanical education. The *Kavyamimamsa* of Rajasekhar, though a late work, suggests that a *shastrakara-pariksha* was held at Pataliputra where great scholars like Upavarsha, Varsha, Panini, Pingala, Vyadi, Vararuchi and Patanjali were examined.[18] Probably, Pataliputra gained educational importance after the fall of Takshashila, the ancient seat of Vedic learning and the 'intellectual capital of India'. It was transferred from Takshashila to Pataliputra where scholars from different parts of India assembled and received patronage of the Magadhan kings.[19] This fact is confirmed by the account of Megasthenes who informs us that at the beginning of the New Year all the philosophers gathered at the Great Assembly of Pataliputra. Briefly, it may be said that by 4th century BCE brahamanical education had become widespread and well organised. It further prospered in the Maurya, post-Maurya and Gupta periods.

Both Panini and Kautilya mention about brahamanical institutions. Panini refers to schools of residential type as well as special schools of *Chhandogya* priests, *Ukthikas, Yajinikas* and *Bahvricas, Natas* as well as rules of education and methods of study (IV.3.129). Kautilya in his *Arthasastra* (1.5.7-8, 17) laid great stress on the proper training (education) of the prince. The entire circle of knowledge consisted of *Anvikshaki* (*Samkhaya, Yoga* and *Lokayata*), *Trayi* (three *Vedas-Sama, Rik* and *Yajus*), *Varta* (practical economics) and *Dandaniti* (science of government. Each of these divisions comprised of a number of subjects or sciences. Kautilya suggests that the child should be taught writing *(lipi)* and numbers (arithmetic, *samkhya*). He also refers to a long list of schools and teachers which existed before him and to whom he often refers. Information on brahamanical education and educational system can also be gleaned from the *Epics* (*Ramayana* and *Mahabharata*) and other contemporary Sanskrit as well as early Pali literature, particularly the *Jatakas*. The brahamanical education further developed under the Guptas due to their patronage to the system. However, by this time Buddhist *Viharas* were emerging as competitors of brahamanical system of education. Though Fa-hien, who visited India in the Gupta period, was primarily concerned with Buddhism, he suggests that the brahamanical system of oral teaching still prevailed and was adopted by the monks also. In his time Pataliputra appears to be a centre of Sanskrit learning where the pilgrim stayed for three years and learnt Sanskrit.[20] Similarly, Hsuan Tsang who visited India in early medieval times during the reign of king Harshavardhan, also informs us about the brahamanical system of education. Sanskrit had become predominant language by this time and was adopted even by the Buddhist scholars and teachers. The study of the *Vedas* was the principal subject of the study. Though Hsuan Tsang suggests[21] that the oral method of teaching still continued, it seems reasonable to suppose that education might have been imparted through written texts also as the art of writing had well developed by the Gupta period and a vast mass of literature existed on secular and religious subjects. However, there is no evidence yet to suggest that the practice of written examination of students prevailed as was the case in ancient China. In fact, the system of written examination seems to have been introduced for the first time in India by the East India Company to recruit Indians to civil and other services. During early medieval times Mithila, the old seat of brahamanic education, again shot into prominence, particularly in the field of *Nyaya* and *Mimamsa*. Kumarila, Mandana Mishra, Vachaspati Mishra, Udyanacarya, Murari Mishra, Gangesha Upadhyaya and Vardhamana Upadhyaya are the most illustrious products of the age.[22]

REFERENCES

1. A.S. Altekar, *Education in Ancient India*, Manohar Prakashan, Varanasi, 1975 (7th edition), p. 235.
2. *Ibid.*, p. 35.
3. *Ibid.*, pp. 259-60. See also, R.K. Mookerji, *Ancient Indian Education* wherein he has traced the development of brahamanic education in *Rg.Vedic, Later Vedic, Sutra* literature, in the time of Panini, Kautilya's *Arthasastra*, education in the *Epics*, pp. 17-344. In a recent study more or less the same stages are marked in the development of ancient Indian education. These are Vedic, post-Vedic, education under the Mauryas, post-Mauraya and Gupta times and post-Gupta times upto 1206 CE. See, Sujata Sinha, *Magadh: Early Education System*, Delhi, 2014.
4. *Ibid.*, pp. 4-5.
5. *Ibid.*, pp. 8-9. See also, Sujata Sinha, *op.cit.*, pp. 4-9.
6. *Ibid.*, p. 588.
7. R.K. Mookerji, *op.cit.*, p. 173.
8. *Ibid.*
9. A.S. Altekar, *op.cit.*, p. 289.

10. *Ibid.*, p. 290.
11. R.K. Mokkerji, *op.cit.*, pp. 177-78.
12. The *Gayatrimantra* runs as follows:

    "Tatsavittur varenyam bhargo devasya dhimahi Dhiyo yo nah prachodyat."
13. For further details of the *Upanayana* see, P.V. Kane, *History of Dharmasastra*, R.K. Mookerji, *op.cit.*, pp. 174-209, A.S. Altekar, *op.cit.*, pp. 291-313.
14. *Ibid.*, pp. 313-316.
15. R.K. Mookerji, *op.cit.*, p. 37.
16. For details, see, *Ibid.*, pp. 77.
17. Sujata Sinha, *op.cit.*, pp. 90-91.
18. Cited in B.P. Sinha (ed.), *The Comprehensive History of Bihar*, Vol. I, Part I, Patna, 1974, p. 262.
19. *Ibid.*
20. James Legge, *A Record of Buddhistic Kingdoms*, New Delhi, 1993, (Reprint) p. 99.
21. For details see, S. Beal (trns.) *Si-Yu-Ki*, Vol. II, his account of the "Middle Kingdom".
22. For details see B.P. Sinha (ed.) *Comprehensive History of Bihar*, Vol. I, Part II, pp. 459-483.

2

The Monastic System of Education

With the origin and development of Buddhism a new system of education–monastic system–developed. The Buddhist *Viharas* or monasteries set up for the residence of the monks soon turned into Buddhist schools for teaching of Buddhist religion and philosophy. Some of them became *Mahaviharas,* the centre of higher learning. It has been suggested that the brahamanical and Buddhist scheme of education was same but marked differences can be noticed in the two. The brahamanical system appears to be something like domestic system of education where the young student received education under the supervision and guardianship of individual teacher. In the Buddhist system home was replaced by monastery where there was not a single teacher but group of monks to impart instructions to the student. The paternal attitude of the teacher towards his pupil noticed in the brahamanical system is not to be found in the monastic system. The brahamanical system prepared the students to enter the *grihastha ashrama* after completing his *brahamacarya* but the Buddhist system did not expect the student to return to family life, rather the products of the monasteries were expected to renounce the worldly life and spend their whole life in spreading knowledge. Moreover, the brahamanical system was not as well organised as the monastic system based on the pattern of Buddhist *Samgha.* Therefore, whereas some of the monasteries like Nalanda, developed in international centre of studies, even Mithila could not acquire the status of a University in true sense of the term.

The brahamanical system did not receive as much patronage and liberal grant from kings and other rich sections of the society as did the Buddhist monasteries. Despite these differences similarities between the two systems may be pointed out as far as the initiation of the student, final ordination, pupil's daily discipline, rules of duties, dress and diet, method of teaching, subjects of study etc. are concerned.

Like the *Upanyana* or the initiation ceremony prevalent in the brahamanical system, the Buddhists also had their own initiation ceremony known as *Pabbajja or Pravrajya*. It literally meant 'going forth'. The person desirous of entering the *Samgha* had to present himself before the order. Specific rules for *pabbaja* were laid down. It marked the period of the noviciate. It applied to all persons whether a layman, householder, wandering ascetic or person belonging to a sect other than Buddhism. The final ordination was done with the ceremony of *Upsampada* whereby the enterant to the *Samgha* was given the full status of a monk or *bhikshu*. The period between two ordinations was twelve years maximum. The *Samanera* (novice) had to express his faith in the *Buddha, Dhamma* and *Samgha* and follow prescribed rules of discipline. He was then placed in charge of *Upadhyaya* and *Acarya*. The *Mahavagga* (1.25-33) makes a distinction between *Upadhyaya* and *Acarya*. Accordingly, *Upadhyaya* was senior to *Acarya*. His main duty was to instruct the monk or *bhikshu* about sacred texts and doctrines. On the other hand, the duty of *Acarya* was to see that prescribed rules and regulations of discipline were followed. Hence, *Acarya* was also called as *Karmacarya*.[1] The Buddhist literature enlightens us on *bhikshu's* (students) daily duties (routine), teacher's duties towards their pupils, food, cloth, personal belongings, rules of begging, games and above all, method and subjects of teaching. The teaching was done mainly orally. The main subjects of teaching were vernacular dialects, Buddhist religion and philosophy concerning *Hinayana* and *Mahayana*. Later on, several new subjects, including Sanskrit and *Tantra* were added to the list of study. Discussions in learned meetings formed important part of the Buddhist education. Although the *Viharas* were open to people belonging to all castes, we do not have much information about the education of women in these *Viharas*. Some reference to the female education may be gleaned from the *Cullavagga* (x.8) where it is mentioned that a *bhikhuni* was the pupil of the *bhikhuni* Upala-Vanna. It appears that separate *Viharas* were provided to the nuns. Such a *Vihara* (Svastika *Vihara*) has come to light from Vaishali (Kolhua). Perhaps arrangement for the education of nuns was made in such nuneries. However, none of the famous *Viharas* and *Mahaviharas* enlighten us on the education of *bhikhunis* in these institutions of higher studies. With the spread of Buddhism *Viharas* began to be established for the monks in different parts of the country, the large number being in modern Bihar, Bengal (including Bangladesh) and Uttar Pradesh. The Chinese pilgrims Fa-hien, Hsuan Tsang, I-tsing and Dahrmasvamin, other Tibetan accounts give us details of these monasteries.

In ancient Bihar *Viharas* were set up mostly in the then Vaishali (Vrijji land) and Magadha. As Gautam became enlightened at Bodh Gaya, the place became very holy for the Buddhists. They congregated there in large numbers, stayed and studied there Buddhist religion and philosophy. Naturally a *Vihara* was built there for the monks. The number of *Viahras* increased gradually. Some of such *Viharas* are mentioned below:

THE MAHABODHI *SAMGHARAMA*

Bodh Gaya, situated nearly five miles south of Gaya, the famous *pitritirtha*, occupies most important place in the history of Buddhism as Gautam became 'Enlightened' at this very place. The place is situated on the left or western bank of river Phalgu also known as Niranjana or Nilanjana. The place is famous for the Bodhi Tree beneath which prince Siddharta attained *Sambodhi*, the Vajrasana and the Mahabodhi Temple. Naturally large number of Buddhists visited the place regularly and *Viharas* were constructed for them. When Fa-hien, the Chinese Buddhist pilgrim and monk visited the place in the beginning of the 5th century of the Christian era, he noticed three *Viharas* (monasteries) there inhabited by the monks. He praised the monks thus, "the disciplinary rules are strictly observed by them.

The laws regulating their demeanour in sitting, rising, and entering when the others are assembled, are those which have been practiced by all saints since the Buddha was in the world down to the present day".[2] Fa-hien does not inform us in detail about these monasteries but it appears from his statement that teaching was imparted there at least of the *Vinaya* rules. However, Hsuan Tsang gives more details of these monasteries. It appears that by the time of the visit of Hsuan Tsang in the beginning of the 7th century of the Christian era Bodh Gaya had developed as an important centre of Buddhist education. He says that outside the northern gate of the wall of the Bodhi tree is the Mahabodhi *Samgharama*. It had six halls, with towers of observation (temple towers) of three storeys and was surrounded by a wall of defence thirty or forty feet high. There was a statue of Buddha cast of gold and silver, decorated with gems and precious stones. He also informs us that this *Samgharama* was built by a foreign king of Simhala (Ceylon). Hsuan Tsang also informs us about the circumstances leading to the construction of this *Samgharama*. It has been suggested that for the convenience of the Ceylonese monks, king Meghavarna of Ceylon (352-357 CE), with the permission of the King Maha Sriraja of India, got constructed this *Samgharama*.[3] When Hsuan Tsang visited the place he found more than 1000 men (priests or monks) living there and studying the *Great Vehicle* belonging to the *Sthavira* School. They carefully observed the *Dharma Vinaya* and their conduct was pure and correct. He also says that this convent entertained many priests of Ceylon.[4] Thus, from the account of Hsuan Tsang it becomes quite clear that there was a Ceylonese monastery at Bodh Gaya where the teaching of *Mahayana* was imparted. The construction of the Ceylonese monastery is also confirmed by the inscription of Mahanaman, a resident of Amradvipa and born in Sri Lanka.[5] A later Chinese pilgrim Hwui Lun who visited Bodh Gaya in 670 CE also refers to the Vajrasana Mahabodhi Monastery where Ceylonese monks lived in good number.[6] During the course of excavation of the site by Beglar and Cunningham, remains of monastery were exposed.[7] It was perhaps one of the monasteries which Fa-hien had also noticed but it had been considerably enlarged by the time of Husan Tsang's visit to Bodh Gaya. Attempts have been made to locate the Vajrasana Mahabodhi Monastery in the Mahabodhi complex. Cunnigham identified this monastery with the remains of mound known as Amar Simha's Fort, north of the Mahabodhi Temple where excavations were made by him.[8] From the foregoing discussion it becomes apparent that by the 7th century of the Christian era, the Mahabodhi *Samgharama* had developed in a full-fledged monastic educational centre mainly for the Simhalese resident monks (Plates 1, 2).

RAJAGRIHA (RAJAGIR)

Rajagriha or Rajagir was ancient capital of the Magadhan empire. It is situated nearly 14 miles south-west of Biharsharif, the district headquarters of Nalanda district. Different names of the place is given in literary accounts, e.g., Vasumati, Brahadrathapura, Kusagrapura, Magadhapura, Girivraja, Bimbisarapura, Rajagriha, etc. Each name has a history and tradition behind it, but we need not go in details of these names. Suffice it to say that being the capital city of the Magadhan empire and Buddha's close association with the place, several monasteries were built here which became centres of Buddhist education. The place finds repeated mention in Brahamanic, Buddhist, Jain literature and the accounts of Chinese pilgrims in the context of kings Jarasandha, Bimbisra and Ajatashatru as well as the activities of Buddha and Mahavira. Fa-hien noticed two monasteries situated in the city built by Ajatashatru (new Rajagriha) including that built by Jivaka, the famous physician of Rajagriha. He also refers to the Karanda Bamboo garden where a *Vihara* was still in existence where several monks lived.[9] Hsuan Tsang also refers to the Venuvana *Vihara* and the Jivakarama *Vihara*.[10] The remains of Jivakarama monastery were discovered during excavations conducted at Rajagir. The excavations revealed elliptical shaped structures with attached subsidiary rooms.[11] The hall was meant for preaching purpose and rooms for the residence of monks (Plate 3). However, neither Fa-hien nor Hsuan Tsang informs us much about these monasteries suggesting thereby that these monasteries had lost their importance after the transfer of capital from Rajagriha to Pataliputra and emergence of several other monastic educational centres in and around Nalanda.

NALANDA *MAHAVIHARA*

Of all the monasteries the most important and famous one was that of Nalanda. Initially established as a *Vihara* it soon acquired the status of a *Mahavihara* and became the world famous University of Buddhist education. It may be called the first Buddhist University. The place was identified with Bargaon located at a distance of seven miles north of Rajgir and at equal distance south-west of Biharsharif, the district headquarters of present Nalanda district (formerly in Patna district). There are several references to this *Mahavihara* in the Buddhist, Chinese and Tibetan literary sources. Long years of excavation at the site have exposed remains of several *stupas* (temples) and monasteries. Several seals and inscriptions have also come to light which throw considerable light on the history of this monastic educational centre. (For details see, Chapter-3).

GHOSRAWAN

Close to Nalanda was another monastery situated at Ghosrawan, seven miles south-east of Biharsharif (Bihar) or eight miles east of Nalanda. Buchanan calls this place as Gosraingya, but possibly he did not visit the place himself.[12] Kittoe visited the place in 1848 but calls it Pesserawa. Later on the place was visited by Cunningham and Broadley also. Cunningham, however, wrongly identified Ghosrawan with the site of the Vajrasana *Vihara*, as it was situated in Bodh Gaya. Kittoe discovered from the mound of Ghosrawan an inscription which records the erection of the Vajrasana *Vihara* by the scholar monk Viradeva. He originally belonged to Nagarhara (Afghanistan). Having completed his studies at Kanishka *Vihara* at Peshawar (in Pakistan), he came to Bihar and stayed at Yasovarmapura. He received the patronage of Pala king Devapala who got him appointed as the chief abbot of Nalanda.[13] Cunningham identified Yasovarmapura (Yasovarmanpura) with the capital of

Magadha and Biharsharif but it is generally accepted that the place actually refers to the existing village Gosarawan which was named as Yasovarmanpura after king Yasovarman of Kanauj who defeated the Magadhan king at this very place. The ruins of the mound have been taken to belong to the 9th century CE.[14] The fact that a monk scholar came to this place from so far a place suggests that Yasovarmapura *Vihara* had acquired fame as a centre of Buddhist learning.

TELHARA

Another important Buddhist educational centre was Telhara in the vicinity of Nalanda. The place is situated nearly 23 kms. west of Biharsharif, in the Hilsa Subdivision of Nalanda district. Locally it is known as Baladitya Dune. It is generally believed that the Gupa king Narasimha Gupta, also known as Baladitya might have contributed to the building of Tiladhak *Mahavihara* in Telhara. In the 12th century Bakhtiyar Khalji looted and burnt this *Mahavihara*. It is said that his army did not move away until the *Mahavihara* was completely destroyed. Fire damaged sculptures, charred remains of food and the seal of Upwasrat Buddha were found from here. The place finds mention in several literary accounts. In the time of Fa-hien Telhara does not seem to be important as he did not visit the place, but by the time of Hsuan Tsang it had become important educational centre and is described in detail by the Chinese pilgrim. Hsuan Tsang mentions the *Samgharma* of Tiladaka (Ti-lo-shi-kia). To quote him, "This building has four halls, belvideres of three stages, high towers connected at intervals with double gates that open inwards (deeply). It was built by the last descendant of Bimbisara-raja (Pin-pi-sha-lo). He made much of high talent and exalted the virtuous. Learned men from different cities and scholars from distant countries flock together in crowds, and reaching so far, abide in this Samgharama. There are 1000 priests in it who study the Great Vehicle. In the road facing the middle gate there are three Viharas, above which are placed the connected succession of metal rings (circles) with bells suspended in the air; below they are constructed storey above storey, from the bottom to the top. They are surrounded by railings, and the doors, windows, the pillars, beams, and staircase are all carved with gilt copper in relief, and in the intervals highly decorated. The middle vihara contains an erect image of Buddha about thirty feet high. On the left is an image of Tara (To-lo) Bodhisattva; on the right, one of Avalokitesvara (Kwan-tsz-tsai) Bodhisattva. Each of these images is made of metallic stone; their spiritually composed appearance inspires a mysterious awe, and their influence is felt from far (or, spreads far). In each vihara there is a measure of relics which emit a supernatural brilliancy, and from time to time shed forth miraculous indication."[15] Hsuan Tsang's account clearly suggests that the *Samgharama* of Tiladhaka was in good condition in the 7th century and an important place of Buddhist studies where scholars and knowledge-seekers congregated in large numbers. During Hsuan Tsang's visit the renowned scholar Pranjnabhadra was head of the *Samgharama*. I-Tsing also observed that it was a very large establishment and provided residence to nearly 1000 monks. The famous scholar in the time of I-Tsing was Gyanachandra. An inscription discovered from the place names it as Telyadhaka or Teladhaka. Moreover, an inscription belonging to the 11th regnal year of Pala king Mahipala I refers to Baladitya, a *jyavisa* of Teladhaka who had migrated from Kausambi.[16] The place also finds mention as Tiladah (Telhara) in the *Tabqat-i-Nasiri* and the *Ain-i-Akbari*. Probably Bakhtiyar Khalji camped at Telhara before conquering Odantapuri. In the time of the Mughal emperor Akbar Tiladah formed one of the 46 *mahals* of *Sarkar* Bihar.[17]

It was Broadley who first of all brought the site to the notice in 1872 and revealed its significance and importance. Later on Beglar and Cunningham also visited the site and did little excavation work. Bloch also did the same in 1902.[18] Since then the site remained neglected till the Directorate of Archaeology, Government of Bihar, took up fresh excavation at Telhara in December 2009. The excavation continued upto 2014. Extensive explorations were made around village Telhara at Ongari, Biswak and Biswa, Islampur, Icchos, Mubarakpur and Afzalpur

Sarunda. These brought to light a splendid tank known as Suraj Pokhar with a temple enshrining the images of Surya and Buddha, two mud forts and remains of Buddhist *Viharas,* mud fortification and tanks. Several Buddhist images were also discovered suggesting it to be a prosperous Buddhist site.[19] The excavations at the Bulandi mound revealed the remains of three storeyed building about which Hsuan Tsang informs us. The structure exposed remains of a prayer hall and residential cells for monks, remains of walls, floors etc. A good number of pottery, several Buddhist images belonging to the Gupta and later Pala period, a stone plaque with an inscription of eight lines in proto-*nagari* script are important antiquities discovered from the site. Sherds of NBPW, Black and Redware and pots engraved with proto-*nagari* inscriptions are notable finds. Nearly six fired clay monastic seals are very important find from the site. On one of the seals the name of the *Mahavihara* is mentioned (Plates 4-8). Four cultural periods were identified :

Period I : NBPW period (C. 6th–3rd century BCE)

Period II : Shunga-Kushana (2nd century BCE–3rd century CE)

Period III : Gupta (C. 4th–7th century CE)

Period IV : Pala (C. 7th–11th century CE)

The excavator believes that after the full excavation of the site Telhara would become as important and famous as Nalanda and Vikramshila Universities.[20] Let us hope that the dream of the excavator comes true.

UDANTAPURI (ODANTPURI)

Close to Nalanda *Mahavihara* was established the Udantapuri or Odantapuri *Mahavihara*. The place has been identified with Biharsharif (Bihar). The tradition suggests that it was established by the founder of the Pala dynasty of Bihar and Bengal, Gopala. Obviously, the *Mahavihara* did not exist in the time of Fa-hien and Hsuan Tsang who do not mention it. The Tibetan sources and large number of inscriptions discovered from the place inform us about the history of this important educational centre (For details, see chapter 4).

PATALIPUTRA (PATNA)

The new capital city of the Magadhan empire Pataliputra was known by different names like Patali, Patligrama, Padali, Padalipura, Kusumpura, Pushpapura, Kusuma-dhvaja and Padmavati in Indian literary tradition. The Greek ambassador Megasthenes to the court of the Mauryan king Chandragupta, calls the city as 'Palibothra', but the most common name of the city was Pataliputra, later changed to Patna and for sometimes Azimabad. Megasthenes gives a detailed account of the city and its inhabitants. The remains of the city of Pataliputra have been located at Kumrahar and several adjoining areas of the modern city of Patna.[21] Besides being the capital city, Pataliputra was also an important educational centre. We have already referred to earlier scholars of Sanskrit literature and language living in Pataliputra. Tradition asserts that the Kushana king Kanishka I took away with him the renowned Buddhist scholar Asvaghosha to Purushapur (Peshawar) from Pataliputra. The Chinese pilgrim Fa-hien mentions it as a great centre of Buddhist learning. Fa-hien came to Pataliputra in search of the copies of the *Vinaya* which were not available elsewhere. It was in a *Mahayana* monastery of Pataliputra that he found a copy of the *Vinaya* containing the *Mahasanghika* rules and copies of other important Buddhist manuscripts.[22] This fact itself proves that Pataliputra was an important centre of learning in the fourth century CE. It was due to its educational importance that Fa-hien stayed for three years in Pataliputra, learnt Sanskrit language and literature and wrote treatises on the *Vinaya* rules. Fa-hien describes about the monasteries existing in Pataliputra at the time of his arrival in the city. He says, "By the side of the tope of Ashoka, there has been made a mahayana monastery, very grand and beautiful; there is also a hinayana one; the two together containing six hundred or seven hundred monks. The rules of demeanour and the scholastic arrangements in them are worthy of observation. Shamans of the highest virtue from all quarters, and students, inquirers wishing to find out truth and the grounds of it, all resort to these monasteries. There also resides in this monastery a Brahamna teacher, whose name also is

Manjusri, whom the Shamanas of greatest virtue in the kingdom and the mahayana Bhikshus honour and look upto."[23] Fa-hien also refers to Brahamana (by caste but Buddhist in faith) Radhasami, a professor of the *Mahayana*, of clear discernment and much wisdom. He was more than fifty years old. He was honoured and revered by the king of the country. Fa-hien goes to the extent of saying that "By means of this one man, the Law of Buddha was widely made known, and the followers of other doctrines did not find in their power to persecute the body of monks in anyway."[24] Fa-hien's account clearly suggests that Pataliputra remained an important centre of Buddhist learning in 4-5th centuries of the Christian era. The situation, however, changed afterwards. When Hsuan Tsang visited the city in early 7th century CE he found the city almost deserted. He refers to the Kukutarama *Samgharama* built by Ashoka, several monasteries and *stupas* but all in runinous condition.[25] It appears that after the decline of Pataliputra towards close of the Gupta period and emerging importance of Nalanda, the scholars and monks might have moved towards Nalanda and its adjoining monasteries. This might have caused irreparable loss to Pataliputra as an educational centre.

KUKUTAPADAGIRI *VIHARA*

We may mention here two other Buddhist monasteries—the Kukutapadagiri *Vihara* also known as Apanaka *Mahavihara* and Phullahari. The Kukutapadagiri is actually Kurkihar, a village situated three miles north east of Wazirganj in Gaya district. Much evidence about educational activities of this *Vihara* is not available but some painted manuscripts, including *Ashtasaharsika-prajnaparmita* were discovered from here.[26] The place was visited by both Fa-hien and Hsuan Tsang. Limited excavations were made at the site by Kittoe and Cunningham. Remains of a *stupa* and monastic cells were exposed here but in dilapidated condition.[27] The most notable find from the place was a hoard of bronze images and metal objects concealed in a room of the monastery. This hoard came to light in 1930. Some of the images had inscriptions engraved on them. These included names of Pala kings Devapala, Rajapala, Mahipala I and Vigrahapala III. It appears that Kurkihar was an important centre of casting metal images like Nalanda and the monastic establishment at Kurkihar existed for a long period 9th-12th century CE but it was also destroyed in 12th century by the Turkish invaders.[28]

PHULLHARI

Phullhari was another important Buddhist educational centre. There is some controversy regarding the location of this monastery. R.C. Majumdar located this monastery near Monghyr (Munger).[29] However, other scholars on the basis of the *Biography* of the Buddhist Tibetan scholar Dharmasvamin and the *Blue Annals* locate it in Magadha near Nalanda.[30] This view is now generally accepted. Much information is not available about this *Vihara* but it has been suggested that here many famous Buddhist scholars lived and Sanskrit texts were translated into Tibetan language with the help of Tibetan scholars.[31]

Although majority of monastic centres flourished in the ancient region of Magadha but some of these were situated in north Bihar also. Of such monasteries mention may be made of those situated in Vaishali and Bhagalpur areas.

VAISHALI

Like Bodh Gaya and Rajagir, Vaishali also occupied an important place in the life of the Buddha. Even before being 'enlightened' he went to Vaishali and met the famous teacher of his time Alara Kalama who was a native of Vaishali according to the *Mahavastu*. Another famous teacher of Vaishali was Rudraka Ramaputra. Later on Buddha visited Vaishali several times, spent many rainy seasons there, admitted women in the Buddhist *Samgha* and even started his last journey for his *Mahaparinirvana* from Vaishali. He also gave his almsbowl to the Vaishalians as a parting gift. It was natural, therefore, that several monasteries were set up in Vaishali. The most important of these was the Kutagarasala where Buddha resided and recited several *suttas*. These *Viharas* existed even after the life of Buddha and spread the teachings of Buddha and Buddhism. An exclusive *Vihara* known as the Svastika *Vihara* was constructed for the *bhikhunis* near Markathrada at Kolhua, Vaishali (Plate 9). It has been suggested that Vaishali was perhaps a renowned monastic university centre with a number of *Viharas* dating from the days of Gautam Buddha.[32] The fact that the 2nd Buddhist Council was held in this city during the reign of king Kalasoka in which several hundred monks participated and the Great Council *(Maha Samgha)* was held, is a pointer to the fact that Vaishali remained an important centre of Buddhist studies at least in the pre-Gupta period.

CHAMPA (BHAGALPUR)

The city of Champa or Champanagara in the old kingdom of Anga, presently near Bhagalpur town, was an old place. The place finds mention in the *Mahabharata* in connection with king Karna of Anga. The place was sacred to the Buddhists as well as the Jains. Chinese pilgrims suggest that there were several *Viharas* at this place. Fa-hien mentions that there was a *Vihara* in which monks were residing.[33] Later on when Hsuan Tsang visited the city he also noticed "several tens of Samgharamas, mostly in ruins, with about 200 priests. They follow the teaching of the little vehicle."[34] However, much information about these monasteries is not available.

THE VIKRAMSHILA *MAHAVIHARA*

In Bhagalpur region the most important educational centre was the Vikramshila *Mahavihara*. The site of this famous monastery has been identified with Antichak, about 6 miles from Kahalgaon railway station. This *Mahavihara* was established by the Pala ruler Dharmapala along with the Somapura *Mahavihara*, presently located in Paharpur, Badalgachhi upazila, Naogaon district, Bangladesh. It was designated a UNESCO World Heritage site in 1985. Our information about the Vikramshila *Mahavihara* is based mainly on the Tibetan sources and excavations conducted at the site (For details, see chapter 5).

Some scholars claim that Naulagarh and Jayamangalagarh in Begusarai district were also important educational centres. Though as a result of limited exploration and excavations Buddhist antiquities belonging to the Pala period have come to light but it is difficult to suggest that these were also educational centres.

Recent excavations in old Krimila region *(Vishaya)* in Lakhisarai district atop Lalpahari in Jayanagar has brought to light remains of Srimaddharmavihara belonging to 11th–12th centuries CE. This is the first hilltop Buddhist monastery of Ganga Valley. Two burnt clay sealings with inscriptions reading *Srimaddharmaviharika aryabhikshusanghasya* (This is the sealing) of the council of monks of Srimaddharma Viahara (monastery) were discovered. The inscription is in Sanskrit language and *Siddhamartika* script of $8/9^{th}$ century CE.

The significance of this discovery lies in the fact that it is the first evidence of a *Vihara* level architecture discovered from Bihar. The only parallel evidence is provided by a monastery excavacated at Jagjivanpur in North Bengal. This is the first hilltop monastic site excavated in Ganga Valley. Architectural features like well preserved interconnected cells, remnants of wooden doorframes, existence of three robust and huge bastions on each side of the monastery, discovery of dozens of wooden votive tablets with figures of Buddha sitting in *Padmasana* in *bhumisparsha mudra* and finally, the evidence of application of red, green, yellow, white and black colours on lime-plastered floors makes the architecture of this monastery the first of its kind on the map of eastern Indian Buddhist establishments. It is the first Buddhist monastery which had a woman monk named Vijayashree Bhadra as its chief. She received donations from Pala queen Mallika Devi. A large number of metal bangles have been also found from the monastic site. The cells of the monastery had unusually doors. It suggests that the monastery was either exclusively for women *bhikhunis* or a mixed one.

The name Srimaddharma Vihara is also equally significant. This name does not find place either in any other epigraphic or transmitted text of the region, but the name suggests prestige the *Mahayana* Buddhism enjoyed in early medieval Magadha. The name also probably signifies close association of the monastery with *Mahayana* esoteric practices, as also vindicated by its very location, atop an isolated hill away from the habitation clusters of Krimila.[35] The excavation is still going on and new evidence is expected to come out.

REFERENCES

1. R.K. Mookerji, *op.cit.*, pp. 395-99. See also, A.S. Altekar, *op.cit.*, pp. 228-29.
2. James Legge, *op.cit.*, pp. 89-90.
3. S.Beal, *op.cit.*, pp 133-135. The King Maha Sriraya has been identified with the Gupta king Samudragupta (335-376 CE).
4. *Ibid.*
5. A. Cunningham, *Mahabodhi*, pp. 42-43 (It is interesting to note here that Hsuan Tsang (p. 135) also says that the Ceylonese king caused his proclamation to be engraved on copper). See also B.P. Sinha, *Directory of Bihar Archaeology*, p. 20.
6. *Ibid.*, p. 43.
7. For details, see, *Ibid.*
8. *Ibid.*, pp. 42-45.
9. James Legge, *op.cit.*, pp. 81-85.
10. S. Beal, *op.cit.*, pp. 152-59.
11. For details of excavations see, D.R. Patil, *The Antiquarian Remains in Bihar*, Patna, 1963, p. 448. Patil also cites A. Ghosh to suggest that a *Vihara* named as Tapodarama monastery existed on the western side of the stream (river) known as Saraswati (*Ibid.*, p. 471). See also B.P. Sinha, *op.cit.*, p. 176.
12. D.R. Patil, *op.cit.*, p. 145.
13. *Indian Antiquary*, XVII, pp. 307 ff. See also, D.R. Patil, *op.cit.*, p. 147.
14. For details, see, B.P. Sinha, *op.cit.*, p. 43.
15. S. Beal, *op.cit.*, pp. 102-103.
16. D.R. Patil, *op.cit.*, p. 562.

17. Atul Kumar Verma, "Telhara (Nalanda) Excavation: A Brief Report", *Journal of the Bihar Puravid Parisad (J.B.P.P.)*, Vols. XXIII-XXIV, pp. 172-73.
18. For details see, D.R. Patil, *op.cit.*, pp. 562-565.
19. *J.B.P.P.*, Vols. XXIII-XXIV, p. 173.
20. For details, see, *Ibid.*, p. 174-76. Recently some more seals have come to light. See, Atul Kumar Verma, *Excavations at Telhara : 2009-2014.*
21. For details of the identification and excavations conducted at Pataliputra, see, L.A. Wadell, *Report on the Excavations at Pataliputra*, Delhi, 1975, (Reprint), A.S. Altekar and Vijayankant Mishra, *Kumarahar Excations (1951-55)*, Patna, 1959, B.P. Sinha and L.A. Narain, *Pataliputra Excavations (1955-56)*, D.R. Patil, *op.cit.*, pp. 371-421 and B.P. Sinha, *op.cit.*, pp. 88-134.
22. James Legge, *op.cit.*, pp. 98-99.
23. *Ibid.*, pp. 78-79.
24. *Ibid.*, p. 78.
25. S. Beal, *op.cit.*, Bk. VIII.
26. Sujata Sinha, *op.cit.*, pp. 173, 181 (fn. 108).
27. D.R. Patil, *op.cit.*, 221-226.
28. Sujata Sinha, *op.cit.*, p. 174.
29. R.C. Majumdar, *History of Bengal*, Vol.1, p. 418.
30. *Comprehensive History of Bihar (C.H.B.)*, Vol. I, Part II, p. 380.
31. *Ibid.*
32. S.C. Sarkar, 'The Heritage of Vaishali', *Homage to Vaishali*, p. 57. See also 'Education System in Ancient India', *J.B.P.P.*, Vols. XI-XII, pp. 62-69.
33. James Legge, *op.cit.*, p. 100.
34. S. Beal, *op.cit.*, p. 192.
35. Information from the excavator Prof. Anil Kumar, Head of the Department of Ancient History and Archaeology, Vishwa-Bharti, Shantiniketan.

3

Nalanda Mahavihara

Of all the *Viharas* of Magadha region, it was Nalanda which evolved in a *Mahavihara* or the seat of higher learning. These *Mahaviharas* (Nalanda, Odandpuri, Vikramshila) are today regarded as Universities of early medieval India. A pertinent question which arises here is whether it is proper to term these *Mahaviharas* as Universities as the concept of University was prevalent in medieval Europe and not in India? H.D. Sankalia has examined this question thoroughly. He suggests that "the word 'University', then has a definite meaning and connotation. It stands first, for a place which imparts knowledge in all the arts and sciences and secondly, for a place which attracted students of every kind from all over the world."[1] The history and teaching prevalent at Nalanda fully conform to the criteria put forward by Sanaklia and therefore, we may term Nalanda *Mahavihara* as University of international repute. No other Buddhist educational institution, Vallabhi in 7th century, Odandapuri, Vikramshila, Somapura or Jagaddal in the Pala period could stand before the fame and glory of Nalanda. We are fortunate in possessing vast mass of Buddhist, Jain, Chinese and Tibetan literature describing the glorious past of Nalanda and excellence made in the field of education. Several archaeological excavations carried out at Nalanda and architectural, sculptural and other material remains, particularly large number of seals and inscriptions, unearthed during these excavations enlighten us on different aspects of this world renowned *Mahavihara*.

LOCATION AND IDENTIFICATION OF NALANDA

Formerly situated in old Patna district, Nalanda presently lies in Nalanda district itself (25°83′ latitude and 85°27′ longitude) and is 7 miles north of Rajgir, the ancient capital of the Magadhan empire and at equal distance south-west of Biharsharif (old Bihar and presently district headquarters of Nalanda). The ruins of Nalanda have been identified with village Badgaon (Baragaon), but in fact Baragaon, Begampur, Mustaphapur, Kapatia, Anandpur and Sarichak appear to have formed a ring of villages over and around the ruins of Nalanda and the village of Baragaon alone can not be said to represent the Nalanda ruins.[2]

Francis Buchanan Hamilton was perhaps the first to visit the ruins of Baragaon (Nalanda) in 1811-12. He has given a detailed account of the place and ruins present there. He says that the ruins of Nalanda are in the vicinity of Bihar, about seven miles west of it. He was told by the local people that the ruins represent the ancient city of Kundilpura or Kundilpuri, famous in the *Epic* and Puranic traditions as the capital of king Bhimaka of Vidarbha, the father of Rukmini and the wife of Krishna. The fort of Bihar was built by the Maga Raja belonging to the Andhra dynasty who usually dwelt at Behar and the place of his worship was Kundilpuri. Buchanan was also informed by the people (the Jains) that the site of Baragaon represented the residence of king Srenika, a Jain and his ancestors who preceded the establishment of the Andhra dynasty here and lived about six or seven centuries earlier. In the time of king Srenika the city was known as Pampapuri. Buchanan also described architectural remains and large number of sculptures, Brahamanical, Buddhist and Jain but majority of them belonged to the Buddhists. He, therefore, took it to be a Buddhist site.[3] Later excavations confirmed the architectural importance of the site but Buchanan's observations that the site was known as Kundilpura and Pampapuri and that king Srenika (Bimbisara) lived here and that the kings belonging to the Andhra dynasty ruled here, are not correct. After Buchanan Kittoe also visited the site of Baragaon in 1847. He also made an attempt to identify Na-lo of Fa-hien with the ruins of Baragaon but suggested that it was actually Giriak which could be identified with ancient Nalanda."[4] It was, however, Alexander Cunningham who convincingly suggested that Baragaon and its surrounding villages represent the site of ancient Nalanda. His arguments were confirmed by the discovery of two inscriptions from the site which bore the name Nalanda.[5] Subsequent excavations have confirmed Cunningham's identification of Nalanda with Baragaon and its adjoining villages. After Cunningham several small and large excavations were made by Marshall, Broadley, Spooner and others. Birendra Nath excavated the site of Sarai Mound. This excavation continued from 1974-82. These excavations have exposed the entire monastic complex and yielded several important seals, inscriptions and sculptures which throw abundant light on the history of Nalanda *Mahavihara*.

THE ETYMOLOGY OF NALANDA

Nalanda is mentioned by various names in the Pali texts and the Chinese accounts. It is often mentioned as Nala, Nala, Nalaka, Nalika, Nalakagrama, Nalagrama, Nalandagrama, Naradagrama, Nalanda, Nalanda, etc. Sastri suggests that Nalanda is a very old name as it was current at the time of the Jain *Tirthanakara* Mahavira and Guatam Buddha in the 6th century BCE. Hence to call it Nalanda, Nalanda or Nalendra is certainly a mistake.[6] However, the etymology of the name Nalanda is uncertain though the place finds several references in different sources. For example, the Chinese pilgrim Fa-hien does not refer to Nalanda but he does refer to the village Na-lo or Nala.[7] It is however, Hsuan Tsang who gives an account of the possible explanation of name Nalanda. About Nalanda *Samgharama* he says "The old accounts of the country say that to the south of this Sangharama in the middle of an Amra (An mo-lo) grove, there is a tank. The Naga of this tank is called Nalanda. By the side of it is built the Sangharama, which, therefore, takes the name (of the Naga). But the truth is that Thatagata in old days practised life of a Bodhisattva here, and became the king of a great country and established his capital in this land. Moved by piety for living things, he delighted in continually relieving them. In remembrance of this virtue he was called "charity without intermission; and the Sangharama was called in perpetuation of this name."[8] Thus, Hsuan Tsang would suggest that Nalanda was named after a Naga and Bodhisattva famous for his charity. Hiranand Sastri suggests that the story given by Hsuan Tsang is evidently an instance of *Nidanagatha* or popular etymology, i.e., an endeavour to explain the name by a story. According to it the word Nalanda is derived from the word *Na alam da* and means 'no end in gifts', or 'charity without intermission'.[9] I-Tsing, another Chinese monk who visited the site of Baragaon also suggests that the place was named Nalanda after Naga Nanda.[10] The Tibetan monk Dharmasvamin gives the name of Nalanda as Nalendra which means 'Lord of Men' in Tibetan. He says that it was built by a former Raja, and because of it was given this name.[11] Yet another explanation for the name Nalanda is given. Hiranand Sastri suggested that the name Nalanda was derived from the word 'nala' meaning 'lotus-stalks' in which it abounded. To quote Sastri, "Even now Nalanda has many lotus ponds which yield lotus-stalks in great abundance and in the season time a number of people are seen daily taking out the nalas or lotus-stalks for sale in the market. I saw this very often during my stay at Nalanda. In that case the name would signify "the giver of lotus-stalks" and "would be quite appropriate."[12] The explanations regarding the name Nalanda discussed above suggest two or three things. Firstly, the place was associated with *naga* worship. Secondly, lotus-stalks were grown abundatly there. Thirdly, the place was rich and prosperous. The prosperity and richness of the place is attested by the Buddhist and Jain texts. Hence we may agree with Sankalia that Nalanda derived its name because of its hospitality and charity.[13]

AN OUTLINE OF THE HISTORY OF NALANDA

The history of Nalanda may be traced back to the 6th century BCE. It seems to be an important religious place where followers of different sects met. It was at this place that Vardhaman

Mahavira who was a native of village Kundalagrama or Kundapura in Vaishali and became the last (24th) *Tirthankara* of the Jains, met Makhali Gosala, the founder of the *Ajivika* sect. Mahavira is said to have spent nearly fourteen *chaturmasas* (rainy seasons) at Nalanda. Buddha also visited the place many times along with his favourite disciple Ananda and stayed in the Pavarika mango-grove propogating his teachings. It is said that Ananda was very much impressed by Nalanda and thought that Nalanda was fit place for Buddha's *Mahaparinirvana* and not Pataliputra. Even after Buddha Nalanda continued to remain an important centre for the Buddhists. We come to know about the developments at Nalanda from the description given by Lama Taranatha. According to him "It was Nalanda which was formerly the birth-place of the venerable Sariputra and it was also the place where he finally vanished from existence with 80,000 Arhats. In the meanwhile the Brahamana village became deserted and there remained only the Chaitya of the venerable Sariputra to which king Ashoka had made large offerings and built a great Buddha temple; when later on the first 500 Mahayana bhikhus counselled together and came to know that they had delivered the Mahayana teaching at the place of Sariputra, they took it to be a sign that the teachings would spread widely; but when they further learnt that the same was also the place of Maudgalyana, they took it to be a sign that the teaching would be very powerful; but the teaching did not prosper very well. Both the Brahmana brothers and the teachers erected 8 viharas and placed there the works of the whole Mahayana teaching." The account of Taranatha suggests that after Buddha Nalanda remained a sacred spot for the Buddhists due to being the birth place of Sariputra. It was due to this sacredness that Ashoka for the first time got constructed a *vihara* (temple). Nalanda also played an important role in the propagation of *Mahayana*. Taranatha also refers to a tradition suggesting that Nagarjuna and Aryadeva were the forerunners among those who took interest in the educational institutions of the place. Suvisnu, a contemporary of Nagarujna, is said to have etablished 108 temples (*stupas* or *chaityas*) in order to prevent any decline of *Abhidhamma*.[15] Hiranand Sastri refers to a Sinhalese work *Nikayasangraha* belonging to the 14th century CE (earlier than Taranatha's *History of Buddhism in India*) which suggests that some Buddhist monks (*Tirthikas*) after the great schism in the Buddhist order after the Third *Sangiti* went to Nalanda near Rajagriha.[16] This would suggest that even before the establishment of the Nalanda *Mahavihara*, Nalanda had acquired the status of being a seat of different Buddhist sects, but the most important being the *Sravastivadins* or the *Mahayanists*. Although Fa-hien who visited India in the early fifth century CE, does not specifically refer to Nalanda, he mentions the village Nala where Sariputta was born and attained *parinirvana* and where a topa (*stupa*) still existed.[17] It is a debatable point whether Nala of Fa-hien may be identified with Nalanda or whether the Chinese pilgrim really visited the site of Nalanda. The description of Nala given by Fa-hien suggests that it was not an important place. Several other arguments also have been put forward to suggest that Fa-hien visited some other place (Nalaka or Nalagrama) in the vicinity of Nalanda. That is why he failed to realise the growing importance of Nalanda.

It was, however, Hsuan Tsang who visited Nalanda in the 7th century CE, gives a detailed account of the establishment of Nalanda *Mahavihara*. The circumstances which favoured the construction of the *Mahavihara* at Nalanda were manifold. Nalanda was very close to Rajgir, the capital of the Magadhan empire and centre of Buddha's activities. The short distance from Rajagriha was of great importance because *bhikkhus* and *brahamacaris* alike lived in places which were a little away from very thickly populated places and yet not so far away that they were not within very easy reach. Nalanda, thus, afforded the facility of access sufficiently. Moreover, other facilities like cheapness, abundance of food-stuffs, its climate, its richness and prosperity, so often mentioned in literature, favoured the establishment of the *Mahavihara* at Nalanda. For example the Jain text *Sutrakritanga* describes prosperity of Nalanda in the following words: "Outside of Rajagriha, in a north eastern direction there was the suburb (bahirika) Nalanda, it contained many hundreds of buildings etc. In that suburb Nalanda there was a house-holder called Lepa; he was prosperous, famous; rich in high and large houses, beds, seats, vehicles and chariots; abounding in riches, gold and silver; possessed of useful and necessary things, wasting plenty of food and drink; owning many male and female slaves, cows, buffalos and sheep; and inferior to no body. This householder Lepa, a follower of the Sramanas comprehended (the doctrine of) living beings and things without like etc. This householder Lepa possessed in a south-eastern direction from the suburb Nalanda a bathing hall, called Seshadravya; it contained many hundreds of pillars, was beautiful etc. In a north-eastern direction from this bathing-hall Seshadravya, there was a park called Hastiyama."[18] The prosperity of Nalanda and the construction of the *Mahavihara* there is fully described by Hsuan Tsang in his *Si-Yu-Ki*. Hsuan Tsang also tells us different stages through which it was built and stood in his time. According to the Chinese traveller the site of the *Samgharama* was originally an *amra* garden. Five hundred merchants bought it for ten *kotis* of gold pieces and gave it to Buddha. Not long after the Nirvana of Buddha, a former king of this country named Sakaraditya (Shikia-lo-'o-t'ie-to), who respected and esteemed the (system of the) one vehicle (the vehicle of Buddha) and honoured very highly the three treasures (Buddha, Dharma, Sangha), having selected by augury a lucky spot, he built this Samgharama. When he began the work he wounded, in digging, the body of the Naga. At this time there was a distinguished soothsayer belonging to the heretical-sect of the Nirgranthas. He having seen the occurrence, left this record: "This is a very superior site. If you build here a Samgharama, it must of necessity become highly renowned. Throughout the five Indies it will be a model. For a period of thousand years it will flourish still. Students of all degrees will easily accomplish their studies. But many will spit blood because of this wound given to the Naga."[19] Thus, according to Hsuan Tsang it was Sakaraditya who laid foundations of the *Samgharama* at Nalanda. Hsuan Tsang also gives a list of other kings who built monasteries at Nalanda. These six kings were

Buddhagupta-raja, Tathagatagupta-raja, Baladitya-raja, Vajra and a king of central India. Thus, "a long succession of kings continued the work of building, using all the skill of the sculptor, till the whole is truly marvellous to behold."[20] It appears that the *Samgharama* established by Sakraditya had developed in a huge monastic establishment when Hsuan Tsang visited Nalanda. Hsuan Tsang gives other details of Nalanda also which we shall discuss at appropriate place. I-Tsing who visited Nalanda after Hsuan Tsang also says that the temple (*Samgharama*) of Nalanda was built by Sakraditya, it had many lofty structures, it was "by far the most magnificent establishment in Jambudvipa. The building is four square, like a city." It was in possession of more than 200 villages which were bestowed on it by kings of many generations.[21] These accounts clearly suggest that in the 7th century CE Nalanda had reached the pinnacle of its glory. It further developed in subsequent centuries till its destruction in the beginning of the 13th century CE.

The kings mentioned by Husan Tsang and I-Tsing have been identified. Of the five kings first four belonged to the Gupta dynasty. Sakaraditya has generally been indeitified as the Gupta king Kumaragupta I (415-455 CE), though B.P. Sinha takes him to be Kumaragupta II (455 CE), Tathagatagupta with Purugupta (467 CE), Baladitya with Narasimhagupta (470 CE) and Vajra with Kumargupta II (473 CE).[22] The identification of the king of central India is somewhat controversial. He is generally identified with king Harshavardhan (606-647 CE) of Kanauj. However, it has been suggested that "in view of the fact that seals of Maukhari kings–Sarvavarman, Avantivarman and Su (cindravrman), all earlier than Harsha are found here tend to suggest that the king of central India could be one of the Maukhari kings."[23] Not delving in the details of these controversies we may agree with Sankalia that the foundations of the *Mahaviahara* were laid by Sakaraditya (Kumaragupta I). Sankalia on the basis of Bilsad Stone Pillar Inscription and Mankuwar Stone Inscription suggests that king Kumaragupta I was a Shaivite when he ascended the throne (415-16 CE) and became a Buddhist later on, his religious views changed between 415-449 CE, the date of the Mankunwar inscription. In order to exhibit his devotion to Buddhism and propagate Buddhism he built a *Samgharama* at Nalanda. This event seems to have taken place in 425 CE. This is the most approximate date of the royal establishment of the monastery.[24] We may agree with Sankalia. Nalanda as a seat of learning emerged in the early Gupta period. It continued to grow in the time of later Gupta kings, the Maukharis and king Harshavardhan of Kanauj in whose time Hsuan Tsang visited Nalanda. Later on, Yasovarman of Kanauj is also said to have accorded patronage to Nalanda University. The Palas, who ruled over Bihar and Bengal appear to be the last great patrons of Nalanda University till its destruction in the beginning of the 13th century of the Christian era. Thus, Nalanda, as a University flourished for nearly eight or nine hundred years. During this long period it witnessed many ups and downs.[25]

Many of the patron kings of Nalanda mentioned in literary accounts are referred to in seals and inscriptions discovered from Nalanda. Seals belonging to different periods and kings (royal seals), monasteries, villages, police station, seals mentioning administrative institutions and units, personal seals have been found in large numbers. Of the royal seals mention may be made of Buddhagupta, Narasimhagupta, Kumaragupta III, Vainyagupta, Sarvavarman Maukhari, Harshavardhan of Thaneshwar and Kanauj, Bhaskarman of Pragjyotisha and seals of Manasimha. A small seal of Devapaladeva (Devapala) was also discovered.[26] The name of Sakaraditya, the founder of the *Mahavihara* is also mentioned in a seal discovered from Nalanda.[27] Some seals are of religious nature and depict Brahamanical deities like Shiva, Durga, Gajalakshami, Ganesha etc., but the most important are the monastic seals. They have been discovered in large numbers. The Monastery No. 9 yielded as many as 690 seals. These were stored in one chamber which must have been the record room of the establishment in that area. They are almost identical. In the upper portion is the Sarnath or *Dharmachakra* symbol and in the lower portion is the legend *Sri-Nalanda-Mahavihariyarya bhikshu Sanghasya*[28] (Plate 10). It appears from the monastic seals that there were different *Viharas* or *Samghas* of the monks at Nalanda. Some of these were:

(i) *Chaturddis-arya-bhikshu-samgha*

(ii) *Gandhakuti-vasika-bhikshu-samgha*

(iii) *Mulanavakarmma varika-bhikshu-samgha* and

(iv) *Varika* or *eka-varika-bhikshu-samgha*.[29]

The discovery of such a large number of monastic seals appears to be somewhat intriguing. Sastri has given a possible explanation for it. According to him, "They were in all probability given to the pious visitors as memontos. Persons who were not rich or could not afford to erect large chaityas or put up costly images got these plaques and then gave them as their offerings. Some of these were given as prasada."[30] Sastri also suggests that "These sealings were needed for being fastened to letters or manuscripts or other documents sent from Nalanda. They would vouch for the genuineness of the documents and might have also been affixed to the certificates 'prasamsa' or 'pramana-patras' which the various educational establishments at Nalanda gave to their scholars to distinguish them from frauds of whom Hsuan Tsang has spoken."[31]

Seals apart, several inscriptions also have come to light from Nalanda which throw considerable light on the history of Nalanda. These include Nalanda Copper-plate Inscription of Samudragupta (regarded as spurious), the Stone Inscription of the reign of Yasovarmadeva, Shahpur Stone Image Inscription of Adityasena, the Kapatiya Vagiswari Image Inscription of the time of Gopala, the Nalanda-Copper-plate of Dharmapaladeva, Fragmentary Stone Inscription of the time of Dharmapaladeva, Metal Image Inscription of Devapaladeva, a Votive Inscription of the reign of Devapaladeva, the Sankarshana Image Inscription of the time of Devapaladeva, the Ghosrawan Stone Inscription of the reign of Devapaladeva, the Nalanda Copper-plate of Devapaladeva, the Stone Inscription of Vipulsrimitra, Buddha Image Inscription of the reign of Mahendrapala, Votive Inscription of the reign of Mahendrapaladeva and Balditya's Stone Inscription.[32] Of all these inscriptions the most important one is the Nalanda Copper-plate of Devapaladeva belonging to the 39th regnal year. It informs us that king Balaputradeva of Suvarnadvipa (Sumatra), attracted by the excellence of Nalanda and through devotion to the son of Suddhodana (the Buddha), built at Nalanda a monastery, which was the abode of the assembly of monks with various good qualities and was white with the series of stuccoed and lofty dwellings. It further informs us that Balaputradeva, through his messenger Balavarmman, the ruler of Vyaghratati, requested king Devapaladeva to grant five villages for the upkeep and repair of the monastery when damaged. Devapala accepted the request and granted five villages, four of which lay in Rajagir and one in Gaya *Vishaya* of Sri Nagarabhukti (Patna division). The four villages of Rajagir *Vishaya* were Nandivanaka, Manivataka, Natika and Hastigrama while Palamaka was in the Gaya *Vishaya*.[33] The significance of this inscription lies in the fact that it suggests not only the patronage of Devapaladeva to Nalanda *Mahavihara* but also of a king of far off land of Sumatra. It also suggests that fame of Nalanda had reached that far.

On the basis of literary and epigraphical evidences discussed above we may summarise the history of Nalanda. Even before its emergence as a great educational centre, Nalanda had become a religious centre. Makhali Gosala, Mahavira and Buddha were associated with this place. Venerable Sariputra was born here and attained *nirvana*. It was the Mauryan king Ashoka who got erected a *stupa* at this place. It was near this *stupa* that Sakaraditya (Kumaragupta I of the Gupta dynasty) built the Nalanda *Samgharama* in or about 425 CE. The descendants of Sakaraditya Buddhagupta, Tathagatagupta, Baladitya and Vajra-added to the *Samgharama* (Plate 11). These Gupta Kings were followed by the Maukharis and Harshavardhan of Thaneshwar and Kanauj. The next important patron of Nalanda was Yasovarmman of Kanauj. By the first half of the eighth century CE Nalanda had fully developed in a monastic establishment, though it witnessed ups and downs also during this period. From the second half of the eight century it received the patronage of the Pala kings of Bengal and Bihar as they had

Buddhist leanings and contributed considerably to the growth of education. Dharmapala, Devapala, Gopala II, Mahipala I, Vigrahapala, Ramapala, and Govindapaladeva[34], all contributed to the development of Nalanda. Govindapaladeva seems to be the last patron of Nalanda *Mahavihara*. It is also possible that the Gurjara-Pratiharas, the Varmans and the Senas of Bengal also extended support to Nalanda. However, towards the end of the 12th century CE due to Turkish inroads in Bihar Nalanda fell on bad days. It is generally believed that Nalanda was finally destroyed by Bakhtiyar Khalji in or around 1203 CE. Dharmasvamin who remained in India between 1234-36 CE, visited Nalanda also and stayed there for nearly six months. He says that in former days it had seven great lofty pinnacles (*sikharas* or temples), fourteen lofty pinnacles (*sikharas* or temples) and about eighty small *Viharas* (*a-ri-kha*), but they were all damaged by the Turushkas (Turks) and there was no one to look after them or to make offerings. Still, two *Viharas* Dha-na-ba and Ghu na-ba were in a serviceable condition. *Mahapandita* Rahul-shribhadra, more than ninety years old lived with 70 monk scholars reading under him. He was honoured and supported by king Buddhasena of Magadha.[35] Dharmasvamin's account clearly suggests that despite massive damage caused by the Turks, it somehow survived upto the middle of the 13th century CE, but it was a mere ghost of its past glory. Gradually it lost its existence also. Several factors contributed to the decline of the Nalanda *Mahavihara*. We shall discuss the causes of the decline of Nalanda later on.

THE MONASTIC COMPLEX OF NALANDA

The monastic complex of Nalanda, consisting of several *Viharas* and 'Temples' was massive and splendid. Some information on its splendour is available in literary accounts. Thus, according to Hsuan Tsang "The whole establishment is surrounded by a brick wall which encloses the entire convent from without. One gate opens into the great college, from which are separated eight other halls, standing in the middle of the Samgharama. The richly adorned towers, and the fairy-like turrets resembling pointed hill-tops, are congregated together. The observatories seem to be lost in the vapours (of the morning) and the upper rooms tower above the clouds. From the windows one may see how the winds and clouds produce new forms, and above the soaring eves the conjunction of the sun and moon may be observed. And then we may add how the deep, translucent ponds bear on their surface the blue lotus, intermingled with the Kanaka flowers, of deep red colour, and at intervals the Amra groves spread over their all shades. All the outside courts, in which are the priests chambers, are of four stages. The stages have dragon-projections and coloured eves, the pearl-red pillars, carved and ornamented, the richly adorned balustrades, and the roofs covered with tiles that reflect the light in a thousand shades, these things add to the beauty of the scene."[36] I-Tsing also priases the *Samgharama* of Nalanda which appeared to him like a city. Similarly, the stone Inscription of Yasovarmadeva gives a beautiful description of the buildings of Nalanda. It is said therein that "She had a row of viharas, the line of whose tops touched the clouds.... That (row of viharas) was, so to say, the beautiful festoon of the earth, made by the creator, which looked resplendent in going upwards. Nalanda had temples which were brilliant on account of the network of the rays of the various jewels set in them and was the pleasant abode of the learned and virtuous samgha and resembled Sumeru, the charming residence of the noble Vidyadharas."[37]

It is quite difficult to ascertain how far these descriptions of Nalanda are trustworthy but the fact can not be denied that the Nalanda *Mahavihara* was a huge structural complex. The archaeological excavations carried out so far have exposed structural remains of monasteries and temples belonging to different periods. It is not necessary to give here a detailed account of these excavations and remains. Nevertheless, a brief survey of these structures seems desirable.

MONASTERIES (*VIHARAS*)

A total number of 11 monasteries were exposed during different excavations. These have been marked as Monastery sites IA and IB, Monastery Site 1, 4, 5, 6, 7, 8, 9, 10 and 11.[38] Except Monastery Site IA and IB, all other monasteries faced west while the IA and IB faced northern direction. The row of monasteries faced the row of temples facing east. Stray shrines were located in the open space between the monasteries and the temples. Monastery site 1 is the most important of the monastery group. As many as nine levels of construction marked by concrete pavements and super imposed walls and drains were exposed here. The main entrance was in the west wall through a large portico, of which the roof rested on pillars. At a later period this portico was converted into a porch with an antechamber. The monastery consists of a number of cells for the monks with wide verandahs in front, originally a building of two, or probably more, storeys. This becomes apparent from the existence of steps (stairs) in the south-east corner. The main shrine of the lower monastery is situated in the east side and originally contained a colossal figure of seated Buddha (Remains of an image of Trailokyavijaya trampling Shiva and Parvati on the eastern end were also seen. Sinha, *Directory*, p. 75). The platform with a number of stone column-bases in front of the shrine might have been used by the teacher to address students seated in the courtyard. The lower monastery, is believed to have been constructed by a king of Sumatra, in the reign of Devapala.[39] Remains of cells, shrine chambers, pulpits, drains, evidence of arches, skylight, ovens, wells, stair cases were exposed from monastic structures.

Generally speaking the monasteries were modelled to be a self contained unit built in the old traditional pattern. It was a rectangular quadrangle bounded by an outer ring of cells around it. The architecture generally follows the descriptions given in the *Cullavagga* (V.I. 3.5.6.) The monasteries generally measure uniformly, 70 x 55 meters in extent. However, the Monastery no. 4 with its annex no. 5 has oblong plan with a width of nearly 40 meters. Nearly 300 cells were noticed in the monasteries. The average size of a cell is approximately 8 to 10 square feet which at best could accommodate two persons at a time. The monasteries were more than one storeyed in height. Each monastery had its own source of water supply. For it wells were provided. Ovens were noticed in some of the monasteries for cooking food but the evidence of community kitchens were not found. Similarly, bathrooms and water closets are absent in the architecture of these monasteries. The only access to monasteries was from the main entrance, which, when closed would completely shut out the interior from the outside world. The cells, it appears, were quite dark or dim inside, there being no opening for light or air except through the only entrance facing the pillared verandah. But as the walls were quite thick, the rooms might have remained cool in summer. The floor of cells was paved with brick or concrete and the roof above was flat, supported on wooden beams and scantlings. Walls were invariably plastered from both inside and outside. In some of the cells built in masonary beds were provided for the monks. There was no provision for keeping any belongings of the monks inside the cells except one or two small niches in the wall, which might have been used for burning oil lamps during night. It was perhaps in this dim light that the monks copyed sacred texts in night with great labour. One of the interesting finds in the excavations is a gaming dice showing that the students or monks, could, perhaps play the game as one of their recreations in the midst of their rigorous life.[40] It was in this condition that a student or monk lived in the Nalanda monasteries[41] (Plate 12).

TEMPLES (*CHAITYAS?*)

The Excavation Reports of Nalanda also refer to several 'Temples'. These were actually *Chaityas*, places of worship by the Buddhists. Why the term 'temple' was used instead of 'chaitya' by different excavators is not explained, but we take the temples to be *chaityas*. Several such temples have been exposed during excavations. These are mentioned as Temple Site No. 2, 3, 12, 13 and 14. Like monasteries temples were also situated in a row facing east. Few temples deserve special mention. The most important one of these is Temple Site 3 (Plates 13, 14). This is an imposing building and the highest monument exposed so far. Seven layers of successive constructions were noticed here. It was a huge solid structure standing in the middle of a court surrounded by a number of small votive *stupas*, many of which were twice or even thrice built one over the other on the same spot. The very small original structure was enlarged by later temples built over and around the ruins of the earlier ones, the present mound being the result of seven successive accumulations. Almost 60 ft. down from the top were found the earliest temple structure built of bricks. It was a square structure measuring 5′8″ a side and revealed no relics. The first three of these structures were small structures. But the later four structures erected from time to time were extensive and constantly raised on higher and higher level from the ground floor. Staircases were provided to reach the top level. The fifth temple is the most interesting and best preserved. It had four corner towers decorated with rows of niches containing well modelled stucco figures of Buddha and Bodhisattva as well as on the sides of staircase. The bricks of the *stupas* were, sometimes, inscribed with the inscriptions belonging to the sixth century CE. On the basis of the stucco figures and inscriptions A. Ghosh ascribed the 5th temple to belong to the Gupta period and the original structure to the 4th century CE.[42] Thus, the earliest evidence of temple architecture at Nalanda goes back to 4th century CE, much before Kumaragupta I (Sakaraditya) built the *Mahavihara* at Nalanda. The earliest *stupa*, therefore, might have belonged to Sariputra as mentioned by Fa-hien.[43] This is the earliest example of a *stupa* or *chaitya* square in plan.[44] The *chaitya* of the 5th temple resembles the *pancayatana* Hindu temple, and so marks an important step forward in evolution of ancient Indian architecture. Perhaps this temple belonged to Narasimhagupta Baladitya. At the north-east corner of this great shrine was a high platform on which votive *stupas* were built. One of the votive *stupas* had a barrel-shaped roof with an arch. It is one of the earliest examples of a pre-Muslim arch made of bricks in the region of ancient Magadha.[45]

Another notable structure is Temple No. 2. It is somewhat different in character and does not conform to the general layout of temples. It lies to the south of the Monastery No. 7 and apporached by the narrow passage through Monastery Sites 7 and 8. Instead of bricks it is built of stone. The most interesting feature of this temple is the dado of 211 sculptured panels over the moulded plinth. These panels are symmetrically arranged, 20 appearing on each side of the main entrance and 57 in each of the three remaining walls. The pilasters intervening between the panels are decorated with a pot-and-foliage design and are surmounted by arches, some of them being pointed. "The theme depicted on panels are religious, secular, didactic like the *Jataka* episodes, comical etc., flying *Gandharvas* and *Kinnaras, Surasundaris,* seated ascetics both knees bound by a band of cloth, a tired man taking respite by leaning on his staff, man fighting lion or fan-tailed *Makara,* cock fight, scenes of archery, snake charmer, lady playing on lyre, the *Kacchapa Jataka,* dancers and musicians, drinking scene, fan-tailed *Makaras,* the story of the talkative tortoise where swans are carrying tortoise on a stick, laughing men, couple in embrace, lady lassoing her lover like a creeper and he is putting a kiss by enlacing her from behind, Ravana (?), three headed, standing next to a seated lady with long tresses, possibly, Sita in a plaintive mood, and the deities like Shiva and Parvati, seated Gajalaksmi, Kartikeya, Rama with a bow and arrow and Kubera."[46] A. Ghosh compares these plaques with those terracotta plaques found in the temple at Paharpur in Rajshahi district of Bangaldesh. He suggests the date of the plaques as 6th or 7th century CE but a later date to the construction of this temple. According to him "the sculptures originally belonged to an earlier temple and were utilized to decorate the present temple when it was built."[47] B.P. Sinha, however, does not agree either with Sastri or Ghosh that these panels were imported from outside. In fact he regards this temple as a Hindu (Brahamanical) temple with sculptured plaques. The temple faces east unlike the Buddhist *Chaityas* facing west. On the plinth, traces of a large shrine are evident. The sanctum was 52′ square externally and had a *mandapa* with its roof supported on pillars and there was a small porch (*antarala*) before it. This is the earliest example of a Hindu temple with a porch and pillared hall. It was constructed either in 7th

or early 8th century in the time of Adityasena. The plinth of the temple contained preponderant number of sculptures of Hindu deities. There are only two Buddhist panels depicting *Jataka* scenes, probably as a token gesture to the large Buddhist community of Nalanda. This temple certainly speaks volumes for the amity prevailing at the time between the two major religious communities.[48]

We may mention here the Temple Site No. 14 also which has yielded the existence of painting in the niches of the pedestal of the image, the only extant specimen of mural painting at Nalanda. The specimens are, however, much too fragmentary and what now remains show the figures of a deer and lion.[49] However, more important are the mural paintings discovered from the Sarai Mound Temple (Plate 15). The excavations were conducted here between 1974-82.[50] The brick temple is very high measuring 31.70 x 22.79 meters. The *garbhagrha* has a huge stone pedestal comprising stone panels in two rows. There are remains of a gignatic Buddha image of stucco in a standing posture on the temple. This Buddha image might be the same 80 feet high bronze image of the Buddha installed by Purnavarman in a six storey pavillion at Nalanda. The temple has yielded a polychrome painting all around the *garbhagrha* hall. The upper portions of the panel are painted with floral and painted designs. The panel below depicts some human and animal figures. Few faces of human figures in red-ochre colour are visible at the upper portion of the white lime plastered walls. The lower portion of the *garbhagrha* has also yielded few floral and geometrical designs, in red, yellow and blue colours. "The most fascinating and interesting feature of the painting is the scroll design depicted on the rear-half of and wall of the temple. This scroll design is very much akin to the scroll pattern carved at the bottom of the famous Dhamekh Stupa at Sarnath."[51] From the temple an inscription of king Purnavarman of Magadha was found. Perhaps this is the temple mentioned by Yuwan Chwang. He refers to a temple of great height constructed by Purnavarman and also of a 80′ feet high bronze image of Lord Buddha. Though the temple did not reveal bronze image of

Buddha but the remains of a gignatic Buddha image of stucco in standing posture on the pedestal was noticed. B. Nath was of opinion that Nalanda paintings resemble the paintings at Ajanta and Bagh caves in technique. He assigns the construction of the temple to the first half of 7th century CE, but he suggests that the upper portion of the paintings were of the last period and somewhat similar to the Rajput and Mughal school of paintings.[52] Sinha does not agree with Nath and suggests that the temple as well as mural paintings belong to the first half of the 7th century CE.[53] It may also be added here that in 2004-2005 close to the Temple No. 3 a number of shrines and votive *stupas* were exposed. Noteworthy among these is the remains of a shrine made of bricks laid on mud mortar in the form of a chariot having spoked wheels in stucco.[54]

Nalanda *Mahavihara* was a very large and massive complex having several monasteries for the residence of the monk scholars and shrines-temples, or *chaityas* and *stupas*–where they could offer prayers and worship Lord Buddha.

THE EDUCATION SYSTEM OF NALANDA *MAHAVIHARA*

The fame of Nalanda rested on being the first well-organised Buddhist *Mahavihara* in early medieval India. Here, scholars and students from different parts of India as well as abroad came in large numbers in search of knowledge. It was a residential University, supported by royalty as well as other rich sections of the society. Though primarily a centre of Buddhist studies teachings were imparted in Brahamanical religion, philosophy and other subjects like chemistry, medicine and even arts and crafts. It had evolved a vast curriculum. Rules for admission, teaching, discipline were well formulated. The *Mahavihara* possessed a galaxy of teachers (*pandits*) of Indian and foreign nationalities. The University was regularly visited by foreign scholars and the Indian scholars also went to different places and countries. These scholars immensely contributed to the enrichment of *Mahayana* and *Tantric* literature. It is rather surprising that despite the discovery of numerous seals and inscriptions from Nalanda, they do not give any information on the system of education prevalent there. Similarly the Brahmanic literature is almost silent on the topic. We have to depend, therefore, mainly on the Chinese, Tibetan travel accounts and other Buddhist literature. They give first hand information on the educational system of Nalanda. Though these accounts may be somewhat exaggerated but we have no other source of information. We have to examine, therefore, these sources for getting an insight in the educational system of Nalanda. Hsuan Tsang is the first Chinese traveller who discusses in detail the education system of Nalanda, e.g., rules of admission of students, the method of teaching, the discipline of the students as well as renowned scholars of Nalanda

RULES FOR ADMISSION IN THE *MAHAVIHARA*

From the account of Hsuan Tsang it appears that admission into the *Mahavihara* was not easy, the student had to pass a rigrous admisson test. This test was not written but of oral nature (through discussion). Hsuan Tsang says, "If men of other quarters desire to enter and take part in the discussion, the keeper of the gate proposes some hard questions; many are unable to answer, and retire. One must have studied deeply both old and new (books) before getting admission. Those students, therefore, who come here as strangers have to show their ability by hard discussion; those who fail compared with those who succeed are as seven or eight to ten. The other two or three of moderate talent, when they come to discuss in turn in the assembly, are sure to be humbled and to forfeit their renown. But with respect to those of conspicuous talent of solid learning, great ability, illustrious virtue, distinguished men, these connect (their high names) with the succession (of celeberaties belonging to the college), such as Dharmapala (Hu fa) and Chandrapala (Hu-yuch).... Gunamati (Tih-hwui) and Sthirmati (Kin-hwui)... Prabhamitra (Kwang-yeu)... Jinamitra (Shing-yeu)... Jnanachandra (Chi-yueh)... Sigrabuddha (Ming-min) and Silabhadra (Kiai-hien) and other eminent men whose names are lost... each of these composed some tens of treatises and commentaries which were widely diffused, and which for their perspicuity are passed down to the present time."[55] The points which emerge from Hsuan Tsang's account are:

(i) The students seeking admission in the *Mahavihara* were expected to possess knowledge of *Vedas, Upanisadas, Samkhya, Vaisesika, Nyaya* and all works of *Mahayana* and *Hinayana* Buddhism. Sankalia suggests that only those students could appear in entrance test who had passed out from other smaller and inferior universities.

(ii) The test was very rigorous, so only two or three students out of ten could pass this test.

(iii) There was probably an examining body of the gatekeepers or *Dwarapandits* to conduct admission tests.

(iv) The tests were probably applied in the case of Indian students only.

The notable foreigners like Hsuan Tsang and I-Tsing did not appear in these tests but were welcomed as foreign dignitaries. We have some information about the *Dwarapandits* of Nalanda. In the eleventh century CE Ses-Rab Byuan-gans was the keeper of the eastern gate, Krishnacarya of southern gate, Ratnakarasanti of western gate and Jetari of northern gate. After Jetari's death Naropa was unanimously accepted as the *Dwarapandit*. All these men were themselves renowned scholars and masters of different branches of knowledge.[56] Regarding the age of admission to the University there was no uniform rule. It has been suggested that the outsiders like Dharmapala and Silabhadra entered the University at the minimum age of twenty whereas the young *bhikshus* joined the *Samgha* at the minimum age of thirteen or fifteen years. I-Tsing informs us that there were students of six, eight, ten, fifteen years and advanced students studying the prescribed grammatical works.[57] This would suggest that the University imparted not only higher education but secondary education as well.

THE LIFE OF STUDENTS

The students at Nalanda University were subjected to strict rules and regulations regarding their daily life, service to the teacher, food, dress and studies. The student's day began with a bath in early morning. I-Tsing gives an account of this bath. He says, "Every morning a ghanti is sounded to remind the priests of the bathing-hour. Sometimes a hundred, sometimes a thousand priests leave the monastery together and proceed in all directions towards a number of great pools of water (near Nalanda) where all of them take a bath."[58] Thus, it appears that morning bath was obligatory for all and there were no private bathrooms. The residents of the *Viharas*-teachers as well as students were accustomed of public bath. The bath was followed by the abulation of the image of Buddha. In the afternoon or in the evening the *Chaitya Vandana* was performed. The period intervening between the morning bath and *Chaitya Vandana* was spent in the service of the teacher, meals and studies. The students had to wear prescribed robes—one double waist-cloth, single upper robe and single under garment. This was eclesiastical or academic dress. The colour of the garment was usually yellow. Perhaps head dress or cap was also worn. We do not know about the use of shoes by the students but they must have used mosquito nets in night. Nalanda was a residential University. Therefore, each and every student was provided accommodation in cells. We have no exact idea how many times in a day students took their meals. Perhaps they had three meals—breakfast, lunch and dinner. The items of meal included rice-water, rice, butter, milk, fruits and sweet melons. During the thirteenth century sour juice of the Nepalese pomegrante was used by the monks as a drink (R. Roerich, *op.cit.*, p. 97). The students did not pay either for their accommodation or food though I-Tsing suggests that the students had to pay for their subsistance. The literary as well as inscriptional evidences point in this direction. Hwui Li suggests that provisions to the University were contributed by two hundred householders from about hundred villages. The Stone Inscription of Yasovermadeva says that Malada, Yasoverma's minister, daily distributed rice with other preparations, curd, ghee and perfumed water to the monks. Perhaps there were community kitchens in every *vihara* at Nalanda where food was prepared for large number of residents. The excavations have brought to light some ovens. The rules of *Vinaya* were strictly followed. Those who violated it were penalised according to the gravity of the offence. Every possible care was taken to dissuade the students from acts of immorality. The standard of morality at Nalanda seems to be very high despite *Tantric* influence. The means of recreation of students seem to be playing of dice. Dharmasvamin informs us that once a group of singers and dancers came to Nalanda and enterained the *Pandits* with singing, music and dancing for which they were paid (G. Roerich, *op.cit.*, pp. 93-94). We may presume that the students of Nalanda also might have entertained themselves by such occasional performances. Poetic recitations also might have entertained students.[59]

THE NUMBER OF TEACHERS AND STUDENTS

Exact information about the number of teachers and students in Nalanda *Mahavihara* is not available. Different number has been given. Thus, Hsuan Tsang says, "The priests, to the number of several thousands, are men of the highest ability and talent. Their distinction is very great at the present time and there are many hundreds whose fame has rapidly spread through distant regions."[60] His biographer Hwui Li however, says that "The priests belonging to the convent, or strangers (residing therein) always reach the number of 10,000." The number of teachers was 1,511.[61] Huwi Li does not specifically speak about Nalanda. However, Sankalia takes this number to be of students of Nalanda as they studied various subjects. I-Tsing suggests the number of students exceeding 3000 or about 3,500.[62] Taranatha suggests that at the time of Rahulabhadra there were more than one thousand scholars, but in the time of Dharmasvamin there were only seventy students. It seems from above that the number of students and teachers varied from time to time. At the peak of its glory in the 7th century CE the number might have varied between 3000 to 4000. Later on when other Universities were opened in the Pala period the number might have declined as many would have joined Odantapuri, Vikramshila or Jagaddal Universities. In the time of Dharmasvamin the number of students considerably declined on account of chaotic political condition and the fear of Turkish invaders. Similar might have been case with the *pandits* or scholars of Nalanda. The exact ratio between the teachers and students can not be precisely determined, but it appears that there were sufficient number of teachers to take care of the students.

GRADATION OF STUDENTS AND TEACHERS

There were different categories of students and teachers in the University. From I-Tsing's account it appears that the students were classed into pages, *manavas* and *brahamacaris*. The pages were the students who arranged tooth-sticks and water and served meals to the *bhikshus*. The *manavas* or the children were the white robed laymen who studied Buddhist scriptures under the priests with a view to become a recluse one day. The *brahamacaris* had no desire to quit the world and studied mainly the secular literature. There were beginners also like Silabhadra who received instructions from Dharmapala Pusa and ordination as a *bhikshu*. However, there is no evidence to suggest that girls or women were also enrolled as students in the University.[63] Similarly, the teachers of the University were also classed into different groups. In the earlier period the teachers in Buddhist monastic establishments were classed into four grades— teachers for going forth, ordination, resources and the recitation of *patimokha*. Later on, the teachers were generally graded according to their knowledge of scripture. Where the spiritual attainments of a scholar were high, he received extraordinary distinctions. The teachers were generally designated as *Upadhyaya, Acarya, Pandit* or *Mahapandit*. The priests were graded as *sramana, dahara, sthavira* and *bahusruta*. An *Upadhyaya* was always a *sthavira* and had passed full ten summer retreats. Names of famous scholars of Nalanda were written in white letters on its lofty gates.[64]

RELATIONS BETWEEN TEACHERS AND STUDENTS

Cordial, even parental relationship existed between the teacher and his student. The student was expected not only to devote his time and energy in his studies but was duty bound to serve his teacher as well. In early morning the student provided the tooth-wood, washing basin, water and towel for the teacher. He also prepared seat for him and offered rice-milk for his breakfast. He assisted the teacher in all the ceremonies and practices of the early hours of the day, cleaned bowls and even sweep the *Vihara*. He greeted the teacher and enquired about his health. Having performed these duties he devoted his time to the studies. Thereafter, he visited the teacher at the first and the last watch of the night again and maintained his apartment, clothes, etc. He was not to accept or give present or wait on any one else, or go out without the permission of the teacher. If the preceptor was sick he was to wait upon him and nurse him diligently. The teachers on their part also had to fulfill certain obligations. The teachers kept nothing secret from the students, taught nothing partially and held nothing back. The teacher inspected his pupil's moral conduct, pointed out his shortcomings and made him repent. The teacher's prime duty was to remove any doubt regarding scriptures from the mind of his pupil. The teacher looked after the welfare of the student and even nursed him during his illness. We have the example of Dharmasvamin and his teacher Rahulsribhadra which reflects the relationship betwen the teacher and his student. When the Turks attacked Nalanda, Dharmasvamin was staying there. To provide security to his *guru*, who was ninety years old, Dharmasvamin carried him and his books and other belongings on his shoulders to the temple of Jnananatha near Nalanda. On his part Rahulsribhadra detained Dharmasvamin for long period out of affection and later allowed him to return to Tibet with tearful eyes.[65] Thus, relation between teacher and his student was paternal and full of affection. There is no evidence of any dispute between teacher and his student. We can not accept Sankalia's argument that "the relation between the teacher and the taught was that of a master and a servant, of a superior or inferior...."[66]

THE LIBRARIES OF NALANDA UNIVERSITY

The University possessed a very rich library for the collection and preservation of original and translated manuscripts. Several manuscripts were brought from outside also. The *Ratnakuta* and *Lankavatara*, two important *Mahayana* texts compiled in a *Vihara* on the Mount Abu, were transferred here. Similarly, a Chinese student Tachi, of Nalanda University, left behind more than 400 new and old works in Chinese at Nalanda. A Korean student wrote several Sanskrit works which were preserved at Nalanda.[67] Being an institute of higher sutdies of international fame, stress was put on the collection and preservation of manuscripts in library at Nalanda. The Chinese sources do not inform us about the library of Nalanda but Taranatha mentions about it. He says that sacred texts were preserved in three shrines of Shri Nalanda (*Dharmaganja*). These were;

(i) Ratnasagar
(ii) Ratnodadhi and
(iii) Ratnakaranda.

All texts of *Tripitaka* were preserved in it. The Ratnodadhi was a nine storeyed building (*vihara*). In this building were kept the sacred text *Prajnaparmitasutra* and *Tantric* work *Guhya Samaja*. These shrines (libraries) were destroyed in fire.[68] Thus, the University had three libraries. However, the archaeologists have not succeeded in locating these libraries.

THE MANAGEMENT OF THE UNIVERSITY

Nalanda being an international University, it was but natural that proper care was taken to manage its affairs. It enjoyed full autonomy in its affairs. There was no pressure from kings or other patrons of the University The University managed its affairs without any external pressure. Another important feature of the management was that it functioned democratically. The affairs of the University were conducted by the monks and scholars themselves residing there. The University had its own seal having the epigraph *Sri-Nalandamahavihare chaturddis-aryabhikshu-samghasya*. It had a large staff to manage the affairs of the University. There were different categories of staff members. The *Sthavira* was the highest priest and enjoyed first rank amongst the priests. Abbot seems to be the governor of the University. This post was offered to priests on the basis of their character, scholarship and seniority. We have the example of Viradeva who was appointed as the abbot (*paripalaka*) of Nalanda by an order of the supreme *Samgha*.[69] Abbot, thus, seems to be the administrative head of the University. Below the abbot was the officer known as *Karmadana*. He is also designated as *Viharasvami* or *Viharapala*. He enjoyed utmost respect. He looked after the general affairs of the University. Hwui Li informs us that when Hsuan Tsang arrived at Nalanda, his arrival was proclaimed by *Karmadana* by sounding of *ghanta*.[70] Probably there was an inspection staff of ten members of the management committee who went around the Nalanda establishment every evening.[71] The academic staff consisted of the *Dwarapandits* who managed the admission of the students and scholars at four gates of the University. Eminent scholars like Ratnakarsanti, Jetari, Naropa etc. were entrusted with the task of admission of the students to the University. There must have been good number of monks to manage the splendid libraries of Nalanda. Besides, there were other persons also to manage different wings of the University administration. Several seals discovered from Nalanda with the legends, *Sri Nalanda-mulanavakarm mavarika-bhikshunam, Srimannavakarmmasthanam traividyasya, Sri Suravi-navakarmma*[72] suggest that the University had its own technical staff of monks who acted as masons, engineers, technicians or architects. Another seal with the legend *Sri Nalanda chivarakosha-thikayatarya-bhikshu samghasya*[73] may be taken to suggest that some monks were entrusted with the upkeep of the monastic garments. As food was supplied to the inmates of the University it seems there was a separate department to look after the preparation of the food. A seal with the legend *Sri-Nalanda satrakasamavarika-bhikshunam*[74] has been taken to suggest that some *bhikshus* were assigned the duty of looking after general kitchen at Nalanda. An important feature of the University seems to be maintenance of punctuality of time. The work of the University was done as per fixed time-table, whether it be prayers, meals or studies. This was essential for maintaining discipline on the campus. For time keeping water clock or clepsydrae was used. Hwui Li informs us that clepsydrae and boys who watched and announced timings to the inmates of monasteries were gifted by kings of many generations.[75] Perhaps the time was measured by shadow also during day time.

As far as financial management of the University is concerned we have no definite information about it. The University received financial support not only from the kings but large number of villages situated around it. Hsuan Tsang informs us that nearly 100 villages were attached to the University. I-Tsing gives the number of such villages as 200. However, the Chinese travellers do not explicitly suggest that these villages were assigned to the University. Possibly they were granted to the university for financial support. The householders of these villages daily supplied rice, vegetables, milk, butter and other necessities to the University. Land grants were also made to the *Viharas*. King Devapala is said to have granted five villages to the monastery built by the king of Suvarnadvipa Balaputradeva. Enriched by the supply of these villages the University became financially sound. It did not face financial crunch during days of its prosperity and provided free lodging and boarding to the students, teachers and other staff members of the University. It is interesting to note here that apart from royal seals several seals bearing the names of villages along with Nalanda *Mahavihara*, district or some other offices were discovered at Nalanda. Some of the clay lumps bear string marks on the back suggesting that these were used for sealing purposes. This indicates some contact between the *Mahavihara* and the villages or the district administration. There must have been frequent transactions between the villages whose revenue had been assigned to the *Mahavihara*. Sometimes the district offices may also have been involved on administrative grounds.[76] Some *agraharas* and *viharas* (*Sri Prathama Sivapura-mahavihariyarya-bhiskhusam-ghasya*, Sastri, *op.cit.*, p. 44) were also attached to the Nalanda University. It may be pointed out that recently a seal discovered from Telhara also refers to Shipura *Mahavihara*. These seals indicate close relation between Nalanda and Telhara. The income derived from these assignments enabled the University to meet its huge expenditure. However, the land grants made to the University entailed additional administrative burden on the University. The University must have regular staff members to manage efficiently the finances of the University.

THE CURRICULUM OF THE UNIVERSITY

Nalanda University had a very vast curriculum. It covered not only theology but language, literature, logic, philosophy, *tantra*, medicine, astronomy and even copying of manuscripts, art and iconography. We come to know about the courses of studies at Nalanda from the literary sources. Some of the subjects were compulsory while others were optional. It also appears that the syllabus varied from class (grade) to class. The lowest class seems to have been made of students who were repeaters of the *suttantas*. The next higher class was of those "who were in charge of the *Vinaya*" which they mastered discussing it with one another. To yet higher classes belonged those who were training themselves as teachers of *Dharma*.[77] Opportunity was provided to the students to opt for subjects of their choice. It was one of main reasons for the fame and popularity of the University. Hsuan Tsang does not specifically refer to the curriculum of the Nalanda University but his biographer Hwui Li says that students in Nalanda study the *Great Vehicle* and also (the works belonging to) the eighteen sects, and not only these, but even ordinary works, such as the *Vedas* and other books, the *Hetuvidya, Sabdavidya*, the *Cikitsavidya*, the works on magic (*Atharvaveda*), the *Samkhya*; besides, they thoroughly investigate the 'miscellaneous' works. Hsuan Tsang himself studied the *Yogasastra*, the *Nyaya-Anusasana-sastra*, the *Sabdavidya* and works on *Mahayana* such as the *Kosa, Vibhasa* etc. at Nalanda from Silabhadra and others.[78] I-Tsing more or less confirms Hwui Li's account. He also refers to subjects like *Sabdavidya* (grammar and lexicography), *Silpasthana-Vidya* (arts), *Cikitsa Vidya* (medicine), *Hetu-Vidya* (logic) and *Adhyatma-Vidya* (philosophy).[79] Thus, it becomes clear that the syllabai of the University included diverseve sbjects and almost every branch of knowledge.

Theology and logic, Buddhist as well as Brahamanical, seem to be chief subjects of study. It must have been compulsory subjects. However, it may be pointed out at the outset that grammar was a compulsory subject of study as Buddhist texts began to be written in Sanskrit from early centuries of the Christian era. The Brahamanical works are not well represented in the courses of study, except the *Vedas*. But the scholars of Nalanda must have been well acquainted with Brahamanical works also to counter their opponents and propagate Buddhist religion and philosophy. It is interesting to mention here that some seals from Nalanda with the epigraph *Traividyasya, Chaturvidyasya*, may be taken to suggest teachers conversant with three and four *Vedas*.[80] Similarly, the root work of grammar Panini's *Ashtadhyayi* and Patanjali's *Mahabhasya* must have formed part of the studies. Logic or *Hetuvidya* was in its formative stage when the University was established. Different schools of thought, i.e., Buddhist, Jain, *Samkhya* and others, had their systems of logic. Naturally a student of Nalanda was expected to learn about all systems of logic as he was expected to counter non-Buddhist systems. With Dinanaga Buddhist logic acquired new form and became one of the chief subjects of study.

Nalanda was the main centre of Buddhist studies. Though *Mahayana* form of Buddhism was dominant here, the study of *Hinayana* texts was not altogether neglected. A large number of texts belonging to eighteen sects and all the collections of Buddhist works were included in the syllabus. Some of these important Buddhist works were *Tripitaka, Prajnaparamita, Ashtasaharsika-Prajanparamita, Yogacarya bhumisastra, Kathavastu, Vibhasha*, Asvaghosha's *Buddhacarita*, Matricheta's *Hymns* and Nagarjuna's *Suhrillekha*. Apart from original texts, commentaries on them were also taught to the students.[81] On logic the most important text was *Tattvasmgrha* of Santaraksita. *Tantra*, apart from theology and logic, seems to be another popular subject of study. Though Nalanda was not as famous as Vikramshila University for *Tantric* studies but the Chinese and Tibetan accounts do suggest that Nalanda was an important centre of *Tantric* studies, especially during the later part of its history.

Tantrayana, Vajrayana and *Sahajayana* developed as offshoots of *Mahayana* and naturally found favour with the teachers and students of Nalanda. The most important works on *Tantra* were *Manjusrimulakalpa* and the *Guhyasamaja*. *Tantricism* not only added to the advancement of religo-philosophical knowledge but also opened up a new field hitherto unknown, namely art and iconography. Large number of stone and metal images discovered from Nalanda were made according to *mantras* or *sadhanas*. This aspect of Nalanda education gave rise to a new school of art called the Pala or the Nalanda Art.[82]

The non-theological subjects of study included different branches of arts and science. Amongst science subjects mention may be made of astronomy, metallurgy and medicine. Perhaps Nalanda was a royal observatory.[83] I-Tsing mentions about an astronomical observatory at Nalanda. Hwui Li also says "The observatories seem to be lost in the vapours (of the morning) and the upper rooms tower above the clouds.... From the windows one may see how the winds and clouds (produce new forms) and the soaring eaves, the conjunctions of the sun and the moon may be observed."[84] Moreover, the use of clepsydrae also suggests that interest was taken in astronomy at Nalanda. It was an important subject of study. Some evidence about the study of medicine is also available. It has been suggested that Gyu-Thog-Yontan-Mgon-po of Tibet was a physician and author who visited Nalanda thrice to study the medicinal works in Sanskrit during the time of the Tibetan King Thi sron-Dehu-bstsan. The medical science contained magic formulas, occult-sciences, medicinal stores, acupuncture and mugwort.[85] Hwui Li and I-Tsing also refer to the *Cikitsavidya* as a subject of study at Nalanda.

The study of alchemy and metallurgy was well developed at Nalanda. The well known alchemist Nagarajuna was associated with Nalanda. Metal casting was highly developed here and it must have formed a part of the curriculum.[86] This hypothesis is supported by the discovery of smelting furnace. From Temple site No. 13 remains of a brick-made smelting furnace situated to the north of the main structure was discovered. The furnace was made of four chambers in one square divided by short walls, each of the chambers being provided with two flues for the fire to burn and air to pass. The discovery of burnt metal pieces, slags of metal fireclay crucibles, crucible lids and other similar objects from the furnace tends to suggest that it was used for casting metal objects.[87] That the art of metal casting was very well developed at Nalanda is attested by the discovery of a large number of metal (bronze) images. These images mostly belong to the Pala period. The Pala school of art is seen at its best at Nalanda and its influence radiated to the east and the eastern archipelago. Nepal and Tibet also closely followed the Buddhist pantheon that was sanctioned by the Nalanda monks. Along with Buddha and Bodhisattvas, images of *Tantric* gods and goddesses were also made. Images of Brahamanical images were also made. We do not intend to go in details of Nalanda iconography but an outline of it may be given here.

Silpasastra was an important subject of study at Nalanda. This *sastra* included the science of arts, crafts, mechanism and other allied subjects. The archaeological remains from Nalanda suggest that architecture, sculpture, casting of metal images and paintings were well developed. Nalanda had scholars well-versed in arts. The names of some *silpis* (architects and sculptors) are found mentioned in some of the inscriptions discovered from Nalanda. Thus, the Fragmentary Stone Inscription of the time of Dharmapaladeva refers to local artisans (of Nalanda) (*silpibhih*) Kese, Savvo, Vokkeka and Vijjata who carved out a stone *stupa* during the time of Dharmapala. It suggests that Nalanda had her own architects.[88] The art of metal casting also developed at Nalanda. Taranatha informs us about two famous artists Dhiman and Vitpala and credits them with having founded a school of sculpture, bronze casting and painting. They belonged to the 9th century CE, when the Pala rulers Dharmapala and his son ruled over Magadha.[89] Whether the two artists mentioned above were related with Nalanda or not is a matter of controversy.[90] However, we may presume that they might have worked at Nalanda as teachers of arts and crafts. Hsuan Tsang (Beal, *op.cit.*,

p. 174) refers to a *Vihara* of brass built by Siladitya and a standing figure of Buddha 80 feet high. His statement points to the fact that the art of metal casting at Nalanda was developed in the pre-Pala period. However, it reached new heights under the Palas along with Kurkihara and Chausa. We may mention here that large number of stone and metal images of gods and goddesses, sculptured panels have come to light from Nalanda. It may be pointed out that under the influence of *Tantricism* the artists of Nalanda during Pala period produced greater variety of images than the Gupta period. Statues and images of Buddhist as well as Brahamanical deities were cast in abundance at Nalanda. The Buddhist figures were of Buddha, Bodhisattavas, Jambhala, Trailokyavijaya, Yamantaka, Tara, Prajnaparamita, Marichi and others in varied poses (*mudras*). Among the Brahamanical images mention may be made of Vishnu, Surya, Revanta, Ganesha, Shiva-Parvati and Durga.[91] As we have already mentioned earlier, evidence of painting has also come from Nalanda, particularly the Sarai Mound. Copying of manuscripts also might have taken a form of art and included in the courses of studies. Sankalia suggests that there is epigraphical evidence to show that the copying of manuscripts was one of the important activities of the students.[92] Thus, different branches of arts and science were taught to the students of Nalanda.

THE TEACHING METHOD

Being an international University utmost attention was given to the teaching and learning at Nalanda. We get glimpses of the teaching method from the accounts of the Chinese travellers. Lecture and discussions seem to be the methods of teaching. In teaching probably the tutorial method was followed. The teacher discussed with students their problems and students also put forward their queries. The students were first asked to memorise their lessons and then discuss it with teachers in class rooms. This tutorial system helped student not only in solving his problems but also establishing a close and intimate relationship with his teacher. This method of teaching is praised by both Hsuan Tsang and I-Tsing. The tutorial system of teaching is well reflected in two panels of the site 2 where in each panel two mendicants, holding a manuscript are engaged in studying and interpreting the texts.[93] Discussion with teachers and other students was another method of teaching. Regular discussions on different subjects, particularly theology, became a feature of teaching. The students benefitted much from discussions. Hsuan Tsang praises this system. He says, "The day is not sufficient for asking and answering profound questions. From morning till night they engage in discussion; the old and the young mutually help one another. Those who can not discuss questions out of the *Tripitaka* are little esteemed, and are obliged to hide themselves for shame. Learned men from different cities, on this account, who desire to acquire quickly a renown in discussion, come here in multitudes to settle their doubts, and then the streams (of their wisdom) spread far and wide. For this reason some persons usurp the name (of Nalanda students), and in going to and fro receive honour in consequence."[94] The statement of Hsuan Tsang suggests that Nalanda was a famous debating centre and any one who wished recognition in Buddhist academic world participated in these debates. We have several examples wherein we are informed that eminent scholars of Nalanda participated regularly in such discussions. Thus, Dinnaga, Dharmakirtti and others are said to have defeated their opponents in religious and metaphysical discussions at Nalanda. Yuwan Chwang is also said to have defeated Simharasmi and established the superiority of *Yogasastra*. There are several such other examples to confirm great value attached to discussions.

Sometimes regular lectures were also organised which the students attended without fail. Hwui Li informs us that "within the Temple they arrange every day about 100 pulpits for preaching, and the students attend these discourses without fail, even for a minute."[95] Even these lectures, very often took the shape of personal discussion between the teacher and the student, who could not follow the lecture or had some doubts regarding some topics in the lecture. The teaching and study was mainly oral. The students memorised texts and discussed it with their teachers. Stress was also put on the chanting of *mantras*.

There is no evidence to suggest that students were assigned written work. The only writing work which they did was the copying of manuscripts, the most important of these manuscripts being *Prajnaparamita*. The scholars of Nalanda themselves wrote several texts, mainly on Buddhist religion and philosophy. This was done not only by Indian scholars but foreign scholars also. Hsuan Tsang himself copied many manuscripts at Nalanda. It was probably due to this fact that Hsuan Tsang could take large number of manuscripts to China. It seems that the copying of manuscripts formed a part of the studies at Nalanda as large number of manuscripts were required by the students and teachers of Nalanda. As paper was not known then, manuscripts were written on *bhurjapatra* and *talapatra*. They were bound together with help of strings. Ink made of different substances was used as writing material. In the Gupta period the *Brahmi* script was used but later on different forms of script, the most important being *Nagari* was used. It may be pointed out that seals and inscriptions of Nalanda do not enlighten us on the courses of studies and method of teaching. How far the evidence gleaned from Chinese and Tibetan sources are trustworthy can not be said with certainty.

An important feature of the teaching at Nalanda was that the juniors and seniors supplemented each other's knowledge in their studies. The scholarship of juniors was given due recognition by the seniors. Moreover, the scholars and teachers of Nalanda did not confine their knowledge to the residents of the *Mahavihara* only but extended their help to knowledge-seekers from other monasteries as well.

EMINENT SCHOLARS OF NALANDA *MAHAVIHARA*

Nalanda had a galaxy of renowned scholars or *Pandits*, both Indian and non-Indian. The title *Pandit* was used in two sense at Nalanda. Ordinarily it meant a Professor. But there was another meaning and that of greater importance. In Vikramshila *Mahavihara Pandit* was a degree conferred on its successful candidates but at Nalanda, it appears to be a distinctive title bestowed on the head of the *Mahavihara*.[96] For example,

Taranatha refers to Dharmapala as *Pandit* in sense of the head of the University of Nalanda. Perhaps the title *Pandit* was bestowed on those scholars who had mastered all sciences. Titles like *Mahapandit*, *Acarya* and *Bahusruta* were also conferred on renowned scholars of the University. For example, Rahulshribhadra was a *Mahapandit*, Chandragomin an *Acarya* and Sri Manjusrivarma a *Bahusruta*. It is difficult to distinguish specifically between these honorific titles, but this much is certain that these titles were conferred in recognition of knowledge and fame of scholars. Information about the life and works of these scholars is mainly derived from the Chinese and Tibetan sources. Hsuan Tsang refers to scholars like Dharmapala, Chandrapala, Gunamati, Sthirmati, Prabhamitra, Jinamitra, Jnanachandra and Silabhadra. I-Tsing, Dharmasvamin and Lama Taranatha also refer to several eminent scholars of the University who were acknowledged for their scholarship not only in India but abroad as well. We discuss here life and works of some of the scholars of this famous University :

Asanga and Vasubandhu : According to Taranatha Asanga and Vasubandhu were *Pandits* of Nalanda. It has been suggested that there were two Asanga and Vasubandhu belonging to the 4th and 6th century CE.[97] Asanga I and Vasubandhu I became associated with Nalanda when it was coming up. Asanga II is said to have founded the *Tantra* school by the middle of the 6th century CE. His several works are available in the Chinese and Tibetan. Both of them made invaluable contributions to the Buddhist philosophy. The *Abhidharmakosa* and the *Paramarthasaptatika* are attributed to Asanga and Vasubandhu respectively.

Dinnaga : He was a great logician. He was a native of Simha Vaktra, a suburb of Kanchi in south India. He is said to have restored the fame of Nalanda when it was on the point of being humiliated by Brahamana logician Sudurjaya. It is said that Asanga was unable to counter the arguments of Sudurjaya. Hence invitation was sent to Dinnaga to come to Nalanda. He defeated Sudurjaya in debate. Later on he settled at Nalanda, studied under Vasubandhu II and became head of the University. His probable date is 6th century CE. He wrote several books on logic. His greatest contribution is that he separated logic from discussion and replaced the word *vada* by *nyaya*. Dinnaga exercised great influence on the intellegentia of China and Japan.[98] His famous work is *Nyayabhasya*.

Jayadeva and Chandrakirti : Between Dinnaga and Sthirmati, we come across two other scholars Jayadeva and Chandrakirti. The name of Jayadeva is mentioned by Taranatha only, neither Hsuan Tsang nor I-Tsing mention about him.[99] Taranatha refers to him as a *Pandit* of Nalanda. He was succeeded by Chandrakirti. He was a 'Master of Masters'. As the *Pandit* of Nalanda he wrote commenteries upon *Madhyamikamula* and *Madhyamikavicara*.[100]

Sthirmati : Another great scholar of Nalanda was Sthirmati. He was a resident of Vallabhi in Gujarat and came to Nalanda. According to Hsuan Tsang he founded a monastery at Vallabhi. Sthirmati had specialised in grammar, was a renowned scholar and is said to have written nine books, translated seven books in Tibetan and revised eleven books translated in Tibetan. He was perhaps the first writer after Asanga to write on the *Tantra*.[101]

Gunamati : Like Sthirmati, Gunamati was also a native of Vallabhi and contemporary of Sthirmati. He enjoyed excellent reputation among contemporaries. He refuted the *Samkhya* doctrine of Madhava and also the *Madhyamika* views of Bhavya. He was the author of *Lakshanasarasastra* and wrote commentary on *Abhidharmakosa*. Several other texts are also attributed to him. Both Sthirmati and Gunamati belonged to 6th century CE.

Chandragomin : He was probably born in Bengal. He belonged to the later part of the 6th or first half of the 7th century CE. He is remembered as one who entered into philosophical disputations with Chandrakirti at Nalanda. He is said to have written a large number of books, the most important being the *Chandravyakrana*.

Dharmapala : He was abbot of Nalanda University. Like Dinnaga, he also came from Kanchi. He was son of a minister or high official of Kanchi. His probable date is first half of the 7th century CE. After Chandrakirti, the *Madhyamika* commentator, he became abbot of Nalanda. He defeated heretics and 100 *Hinayani* scholars in disputation. He acquired renown for penetration and wisdom and the reputation of his noble character was far-spread. He wrote several books and commentaries on etymology, logic and metaphysics. One of his important works is *Sabdavidyasamyuktasastra*. His work the *Satasastravaipulayavyakhya* was translated into Chinese.

Silabhadra : Silabhadra was another renowned scholar of Nalanda. He belonged to the royal brahamana family of Samatata. At Nalanda he was initiated into Buddhism by Dharmapala. He was contemporary of Hsuan Tsang. He is said to have defeated a south Indian brahmana heretic and was granted ravenues of a village by the king of Magadha, despite his persistant refusal. He, however, built a monastery out of this revenue. This monastery lay somewhere on the route from Patna to Gaya.[102] From a mere disciple of Dharmapala he rose to the status of the head of Nalanda University. It was during his time that Hsuan Tsang visited Nalanda. Silabhadra made elaborate arrangements to accord warm reception to Hsuan Tsang. The Chinese pilgrim studied *Yogasastra* under his supervision. It was also on his direction that Hsuan Tsang visited the court of Harshavardhan and the king of Kamarupa. Silabhadra's profound knowledge, his virtue and advanced age earned for him the title of the *pater familias* of the Buddhist community.[103] He is said to have died at the age of 106 years.[104] The only work assigned to him is the *Aryabuddhabhumi Vyakhyana* preserved in the Tibetan, though it is possible that he might have written several other books.

Saraha Rahulabhadra : He was the predecessor of Nagarjuna in the abbot's chair of Nalanda. Sarha taught Nagarjuna the *Guhyasamjatantra*. He is said to have converted a king with 5000 people to Buddhism. He was a reputed teacher of Sanskrit at Nalanda. Sixteen works in *Maghi*, translated into Tibetan, are attributed to him. He composed *dohas*, the *Dohakosa-giti* and the *Charyagiti* in *Apbhramsa* with a Sanskrit commentary.[105]

Nagarjuna II : We get reference to many Nagarjunas, at least five from time to time. Of these, Nagarjuna the *siddha*, appears to be connected with Nalanda. He hailed from South India and belonged to the 7th century CE. He studied *Guhyasamaja* with his teacher Sarha Rahulabhadra. He obtained an elixir-producing gold and arranged meals for the monks of Nalanda during a famine. Yuwan-Chwang refers to the transformation of rocks into gold by Nagarjuana. He was famous as a great alchemist. He was author of several books, the most important being *Suhrillekha*.[106] He became abbot of Nalanda after Saraha.

Santideva : The *Buddha-Gana-o-Doha* preserves an account of the life of Santideva. He belonged to a royal family of Saurashtra. His probable date is 7th century CE. Important texts attributed to him are the *Sikshasamuchchaya*, the *Sutrasamuchchaya* and *Bodhicharyavatara*.

Santarakshita : Santarakshita was another great scholar of Nalanda *Mahavihara*. He was a great philosopher, logician and *Tantric*. He lived in the first half of the 8th century CE. There is some controversy regarding his native place. Some regard him as the inhabitant of Zahor (Jessore), Sahor in Bhagalpur district or Sahor in the north-west country corner of Andhra country.[107] He was the high priest of Nalanda *Mahavihara* and probably the spiritual teacher of the king of Magadha. He had the distinction of being the first *Pandit* of Nalanda who was officially invited to Tibet by King Khir-son-den-stan. He spent a good part of his life in Tibet. On his request the king also invited Padmasambha, another scholar of Nalanda, to Tibet. In 749 CE, Santarakshita and Padamasambha got constructed a monastery in Tibet. This monastery known as "Sam-ye" was modelled on the Odantapuri monastery. Santarakshita became the first abbot of this monastery.[108] Santarakshita spent the rest of his life in Tibet and propagated the Buddhist philosophy. He is credited with having written several texts and translated some Sanskrit texts into Tibetan. His most important work is *Tattvasangraha,* an encyclopaedic work dealing with theology, philosophy, logic and grammar.

Padmasambhava : As indicated above, he was a contemporary of Santarakshita and worked with him in Tibet. He was one of renowned *Tantric* teachers of Nalanda University. He was probably son of king Indrabhuti of Udyana (Swat) in Afghanistan, a native of Ghazni or belonged to Andhra country. He was master of astrology, medicine, language, arts and crafts. He was a prominent expounder of the *Yogacara* school. His famous book is *Samayapanchaska* in Tibetan. He founded *Lamaism* in Tibet and is regarded as the Buddha himself in *Lamaism.*

Kamalasila : He was also a great *Tantric* teacher of Nalanda. He also went to Tibet on the invitation of the Tibetan king and defeated there the Chinese scholar Hoshang in debate. He translated several Sanskrit works in Tibetan and wrote *Panjika,* a commentary on the *Tattvasangraha* written by Santarakshita.

Viradeva : The Ghosrawan Stone Inscription of the reign of king Devapala[109] of the Pala dynasty informs us about this scholar. He was a resident of Nagarahara (Jalalabad) in Uttarapatha. His father's name was Indragupta, who belonged to a respectable and prosperous family. Having studied at Kanishka *Vihara* (Peshawar) he visited Vajrasana (Bodh Gaya) and finally came to Yasovarmapura *Vihara* near Nalanda. Viradeva perhaps came to Nalanda, thinking that it was the only place in India which would recognise his merits and honour him accordingly. His dreams came true when being impressed by his scholarship Devapala got him appointed by the *Bhikshu-samgha* as governor of Nalanda *Mahavihara.*

Dipankarasrijnan Atisa : Atisa belonged to a royal family, either of Bengal or Bhagalpur. Having studied first at Vikramshila he came to Nalanda. He was a great scholar. He studied at different places, Vikramshila, Vajrasana, and went to Suvarnadvipa and Tibet. He died near Lhasa in Tibet. He is said to have written more than 200 books. Many of his books were translated into Tibetan. One of his important text is *Taratriratnastrotam*.

Buddhakirti : He was a distinguished scholar. "In him we find the last connecting link between the Universities of Nalanda and Vikramshila and he was perhaps the last great scholar that the University produced before it was destroyed by the Moslems."[110] He was a contemporary of Abhyankaragupta of Vikramshila University.

Apart from scholars mentioned above, there were several other great scholars associated with Nalanda *Mahavihara*, who enhanced its fame and glory. In this connection mention may be made of Dharmakirti, Manjusrivarma, Jetari, Vagisvarakirti, Ratnakarasanti, Tilopa and Naropa. Rahulshribhadra appears to be the last great scholar of Nalanda. It was during his times that the Tibetan monk Dharmasvamin came to Nalanda. He was more than ninety years old when Dharmasvamin visited Nalanda. By this time the glory of Nalanda had faded and there were few Buddhist monks there. There was constant threat of the Turkish invasion.[111]

The scholars of Nalanda were regarded as role models of simple living, high knowledge and thinking and strict disciplinaries in India as well as abroad.

THE CHINESE AND OTHER SCHOLARS AT NALANDA

Not only students and scholars from different corners of India came to Nalanda, stayed there and studied Buddhist religion, philosophy, logic and *Tantra* but a large number of foreigners also came to this *Mahavihara*. They came from China, Tibet, Korea and even Afghanistan. Among the Chinese scholars names of Hsuan Tsang and I-Tsing stand out prominently.

Hsuan Tsang (Yuan Chwang) : Hsuan Tsang was born in 603 CE at Chin Liu, in the province of Ho-nan, in China. He came to India in 629 CE and returned to China in 645 CE. After covering a long distance he reached Nalanda in 637 CE and stayed there for five years. During his stay at Nalanda king Siladitya (Harshavardhan) was on the throne of Kanauj. He learnt Sanskrit and *Yogasastra* from his *guru* Silabhadra. He visited Hrshavardhan's court and the king of Kamarupa (Assam). He is one of the most respectable scholars of his time. His biographer Hwui Li gives a graphic description of his stay at Nalanda. After his return to China he wrote his travelogue known as *Si-Yu-Ki*. While at Nalanda he participated in several disputations and came victorious over his opponents. He refuted the *Hinayana* heretics of Orissa also. He was famous as 'Master of the Law'. He wrote several books and translated large number of Sanskrit texts into Chinese (nearly 657). Some of these works were the *Abhidharmakosa* and the *Mahaprajnaparamitasutra*.

While returning to China he carried with him "Five hundred grains of relics belonging to the body (flesh) of Tathagata, a golden statue of Buddha on a transparent pedestal, a statue of Buddha carved out of sandal wood on a transparent pedestal.... One hundred and twenty four works (Sutras) of the Great Vehicle, other works, amounting in the whole to 520 fasciculi, carried by twenty-two horses".[112]

I-Tsing : Another renowned scholar, probably the most famous Chinese after Hsuan Tsang, was I-Tsing. He was born at Panyang in China. He came to Nalanda from Vajrasana with twenty monks in 671 or 675 CE and stayed and studied there for nearly ten years. He has given a detailed and interesting account of Hsuan Tsang's visit to Nalanda and reception accorded to him. He also informs us about other aspects of Nalanda University. He is said to have translated the *Mulasarvastivada-nikayavinayagatha* into Chinese. He returned to China via Tamralipti, taking with him Indian texts of more than 500,000 *slokas* and a real plan of the Vajrasana.[113]

Apart from Hsuan Tsang and I-Tsing several other Chinese monks and scholars like Wu-Hing, Yuan-Chau, Tcha-Hong, Tao-Hi (Srideva) visited Nalanda and studied there. Similarly nearly six Koreans came to Nalanda.[114] Bodhidharma from Tukhara country also visited Nalanda.[115] We have information about Tibetans also at Nalanda University though their number was lesser than at Vikramshila. Mention may be made of Thon-Mi

Sambhota, Gyu-Thog-Yontan-Mgon-Po and most notably Dharmasvamin. Dharmasvamin came to Nalanda in and around 1236 CE and became a trustworthy disciple of Rahulasribhadra. He was well versed in *Tantra*, grammar, philosophy and Sanskrit. He translated nearly thirty works into Tibetan.

NALANDA SCHOLARS ABROAD

Nalanda not only received foreign students and scholars but it also sent its scholars to China, Tibet, Korea, Japan and Ceylon to spread the teachings of Buddha and establish superiority of *Mahayana*. The scholars of Nalanda were in close contact with China and Tibet. Prabhakaramita went to China via Iran in 627 CE. He translated three Buddhist works there. The Chinese scholars became jealous of him due to high honours bestowed on him. He was perhaps the first scholar of Nalanda to reach China via Tibet. Vajrabodhi along with his disciple Amoghavajra reached China via Ceylon. He propoagated *Tantrayana* there and translated eleven *Tantric* works into Chinese. He propagated and deepend the roots of the *Guhya-cult* in China. He translated nearly seventy-seven texts into Chinese. Another famous scholar of Nalanda to visit China was Subhakarasimha. He is said to have established in China the *Guhya* school and translated several texts into Chinese. Munisri was another scholar to go to China.[116] All these scholars went to China in 7-8th centuries CE. In 9th and 10th centuries, however, due to political chaos prevailing in China, it became somewhat difficult for Indian scholars to go there. However, from the later part of 10th century CE Indian scholars again began their journey to China. The most important scholar of Nalanda to go to China in the later part of the 10th century CE was Dharmadeva. He was one of the most famous translators of the Song Dynasty and was appointed a member of the Imperial Board for the translation of Indian Buddhist texts.[117] He translated nearly forty six texts, the most important being the *Sukhavativyuha*. In appreciation of his scholarship and works he was conferred the title of "Kwhan Kai-tash" by the Chinese Emperor Theitsun. In order to encourage other scholars to work like Dharmadeva, the Chinese Emperor bestowed another title "Hhuien Kiao Shah" posthumously to Dharmadeva.[118] In later period also several Indian scholars went to China and impressed the Chinese by their scholarship. Tibet was another destination of Indian scholars. We have already discussed the works of Santarakshita, Padmasambhava, Kamalsila, Dipankarasrijna Atisa in Tibet and need not repeat it here. While majority of Indian scholars went to China and Tibet, some visited Ceylon, Suvarnadvipa and even Korea. Dharmapala and Atisa also visited Suvarnadvipa. Thus, the scholars and teachers of Nalanda spread their fame in foreign land as well.

THE INTERNATIONAL CHARACTER OF THE *MAHAVIHARA*

Nalanda *Mahavihara* was not only a full-fledged Indian University but international University as well. It had close relation with other contemporary Indian Universities like Vallabhi, Vajrasana, Odantapuri, Vikramshila, Somapura and Jagaddal. There was close contact between Nalanda and these universities. Scholars and students from other Universities came to Nalanda in search of knowledge as none of these Universities could rival Nalanda, not even Vallabhi and Vikramshila. Both Hsuan Tsang and I-Tsing praise Vallabhi. I-Tsing even goes to the extent of saying that Vallabhi was as great and famous as Nalanda. He compares Nalanda and Vallabhi to Chinma, Shih-chu, Lungmen and Chiue-li, all famous Universities of China.[119] Both Nalanda and Vallabhi were contemporary. We have evidence to show that Sthirmati and Gunmati came to Nalanda from Vallabhi. Though Vallabhi University established by the Maitrakas, championed the cause of *Hinyana* Buddhism it also imparted teaching of *niti, varta* and other allied subjects. The University flourished between 600 CE and 1200 CE. Gunmati and Sthiramati were two eminent scholars of Vallabhi. Viradeva, having completed his studies at Peshawar came to Somapura *Mahavihara* and from there went to Nalanda. There was also close connection between Odantpuri and Vikramshila. When the Universities of Odantapuri, Vikramshila, Jagddal and Somapura *Mahaviharas* were established by the Palas of Bihar and Bengal, close contacts developed between Nalanda and these Universities. For example, Naropa had the honour of being gatekeeper of both Nalanda and Vikramshila Universities. There are several other references to indicate close connection between Odantpuri, Nalanda and Vikramshila Universities. Thus, during the period of its existence Nalanda had become the all India centre of higher learning. Similarly, there was exchange of scholars between China and Tibet. Both China, Tibet and India contributed immensely to the Buddhist and *Tantric* studies. Nalanda also developed relations with other south-east Asian countries and in true sense became the first international University.

REFERENCES

1. H.D. Sankalia, *The University of Nalanda*, Delhi, 1972 (2nd revised and enlarged edition), p. 2.
2. B.N. Mishra, *Nalanda*, Vol. I, Delhi 2008 (2nd edn.), p. 163. It may be mentioned here that D.R. Patil (*The Antiquarian Remains in Bihar*, Patna, 1963, p. 300) refers to villags Jagadispur and Muzaffarpur also surrounding Baragaon.
3. For details see, Francis Buchanan, *An Account of the Districts of Bihar and Patna*, pp. 219 ff, *Patna and Gaya*, pp. 220 ff.
4. *Journal of the Asiatic Society of Bengal (JASB)*, 1847, pp. 954 ff.
5. Cunningham, *Archaeological Survey of India Report*, Vol. I, p. 28 ff.
6. Hiranand Sastri, *Nalanda And Its Epigraphical Material*, Delhi, 1986 (Reprint), p. 3.
7. James Legge, *A Record of Buddhistic Kingdoms*, p. 81.
8. S. Beal, *Buddhist Records of the Western World*, Vol. II, pp. 167-68.
9. Hiranand Sastri, *op.cit.*, pp. 3-4. See also, H.D. Sankalia, *op.cit.*, p. 38.
10. *Journal of the Royal Asiatic Society (New series)*, XXX (1881), p. 571.
11. G. Roerich (trns.), *Biography of Dharmasvamin*, p. 90.
12. Hiranand Sastri, *op.cit.*, p. 4, D.R. Patil, *The Antiquarian Remains in Bihar* (pp. 306-307) however, doubts whether tanks or ponds really existed before the name was given to the place. According

to him many of them were probably excavated afterwards to provide for the required material of earth for the manufacture of the enormous quantity of bricks needed to raise the numerous buildings of Nalanda from time to time. It may also be pointed out here that on the basis of Ceylonese evidence, Sastri (*op.cit.*, p. 3) suggested that 'Na' in Nalanda means iron-wood tree and the name might be interpreted as 'a high ground with low jungle of iron-wood trees'.

13. For details of the Buddhist and Jain texts referring to the prosperity of Nalanda see, Sankalia, *op.cit.*, pp. 39-40, Hiranand Sastri, *op.cit.*, pp. 4-14.
14. Taranatha, *History of Buddhism in India*, p. 72.
15. *Ibid.*
16. Hiranand Sastri, *op.cit.*, p. 13.
17. James Legge, *op.cit.*, p. 81.
18. *Sutrakritanga* cited in Hiranand Sastri, *op.cit.*, p. 9.
19. S. Beal, *op.cit.*, p. 168.
20. *Ibid.*, pp. 168-170.
21. For details see, H.D. Sankalia, *op.cit.*, p. 50, Hiranand Sastri, *op.cit.*, p. 17.
22. For the identification of these Gupta kings see, H.D. Sankalia, *op.cit.*, pp. 52-56. See also, B.P. Sinha, *Decline of the Kingdom of Magadha, The Comprehensive History of Bihar*, (Ed.), Vol. I, pt. II and H.C. Roychauduri, *Political History of Ancient India.*
23. B.P. Sinha, *Directory of Bihar Archaeology*, p. 66.

    It may be pointed out here that the identification and date of the kings mentioned by Hsuan Tsang is somewhat controversial. Different views have been expressed in this connection. For different views see, B.N. Mishra, *Nalanda*, Vol. I, pp. 181-197.
24. H.D. Sankalia, *op.cit.*, pp. 56-57.
25. B.N. Mishra suggests that Nalanda received attention of its patrons till the 15 century CE and even beyond that period. According to him the Senas of Bengal and the Pithipatis of Magadha as well as Chagalaraja, also known as Raja Ganesha (1396-1414) "rendered great revernce" to the Nalanda temple and his queen patronised repairs to the ruined monastries of Nalendra

(Nalanda). During 16th century Nalanda came to be known as Badgama (Baragaon) and became chief centre of Jainism and Brahamanisim. See, *Ibid.*, pp. 182-2013.

26. For details see, Hiranand Sastri, *op.cit.*, pp. 26-72.

    For Devapala's seal see, *ibid.* (*Sri Devapala-gandhakudyam (tyam).*

27. *Ibid.*, p. 38 (S.I. 848)

    I. *(nda)yam Sri Sakraditya-karita*

    II. *hare chaturddisiy-arya-ma(ma)ha*

    III. *bhikshusanghasya.*

28. *Ibid.*, p. 36

    I. *Sri-Nalanda-Maha*

    II. *Vihariy-arya-bhi*

    III. *kshu-sanghasya*

29. *Ibid.*, 27 See also p. 37 ff.

30. *Ibid.*, p. 76.

31. *Ibid.*, p. 27

32. *Ibid.*, pp. 77-107. See also D.R. Patil, *op.cit.*, pp. 331-334.

33. For text and translation of this inscription see, Hiranand Sastri, *op.cit.*, pp. 92-102.

34. For a good account of the history of the Palas in Bihar, see B.P. Sinha, (ed.). *Comprehensive History of Bihar*, Vol. I, II, pp. 245-272.

35. G. Roerich, *op.cit.*, pp. XIX-XX, 90-91.

36. S. Beal (trns.), *The Life of Hiuen Tsiang by Hwui-Li*, Delhi, 1973 (Reprint), pp. 111-112.

37. Hiranand Sastri, *op.cit.*, p. 81.

38. A. Ghosh, *Nalanda*, Archaeological Survey of India, New Delhi, 2006 (7th edn.), pp. 19-30. B.P. Shina, however, *op.cit.*, p. 73, gives the number of monasteries as 13.

39. *Ibid.*, pp. 20-22.

40. D.R. patil, *op.cit.*, p. 324.

41. For a good and detailed account of the monasteries of Nalanda see, B.N. Mishra, *op.cit.*, Vol. 3, pp. 195-218, D.R. Patil, *op.cit.*, pp. 312-324, C.S. Upasaka (ed.), *Nalanda: Past and Present*, Nava

Nalanda Mahavihara, Nalanda, 1977, pp. 65-76, B.P. Sinha, *Directory*, pp. 73-77, A Ghosh, *op.cit.*, pp. 19-30.

42. A. Ghosh, *op.cit.*, pp. 17-18.
43. C.S. Upasaka, *op.cit.*, p. 77.
44. B.P. Sinha, *Directory*, p. 68.
45. *Ibid.*, pp. 69-70.
46. C.S. Upasaka, *op.cit.*, Hirand Sastri, *op.cit.*, pp. 25-26.
47. A. Ghosh, *op.cit.*, pp. 33-34. Sastri regards these panels as Brahamanical and suggests like Ghosh that these must have come from outside, see, Sastri, *op.cit.*, p. 26.
48. For details, see, B.P. Sinha, *Directory*, pp. 72-73.

    Hiranand Sastri, *op.cit.*, p. 83. Hiranand Sastri had also suggested about the Brahamanical influence at Nalanda. The Shahpur Stone Image Inscription of Adityasena of the Harsha era 66 (672-736 CE) refers to Nalanda as an *agrahara*. There are several other seals found from Nalanda which mention *agrahara* in lieu of a monastery and bear symbols which are more of a Brahamanical than Buddhistic nature. Thus, "Nalanda was not an exclusively Buddhist habitation but must have had Brahmanical establishments also in the 7th century after Christ," see, Hiranand Sastri, *op.cit.*, p. 83.
49. A. Ghosh, *op.cit.*, p. 32.
50. For details, see, B. Nath, *Nalanda Murals*, 1983.
51. *Ibid.*, pp. XXIII-XXIV.
52. *Ibid.*, p. 51.
53. B.P. Sinha, *Directory*, pp. 78-80.
54. A. Ghosh, *op.cit.*, p. 57.
55. S. Beal, *op.cit.*, pp. 171-172. See also, *The Life of Hsuan Tsang*, p. 121. I-Tsing also corroborates Hsuan Tsang's account. See also, J. Takakusu (trns.) *A Record of the Buddhist Religion*.
56. B.N. Mishra, *op.cit.*, Vol. I, pp. 237, 240-41.
57. *Ibid.*, p. 241
58. J. Takakusu, *op.cit.*, pp. 108-09.
59. For details of student life at Nalanda see, H.D. Sankalia, *op.cit.*, Chapter VII.

60. S. Beal, *op.cit.*, p. 170.

61. *Life*, p. 112.

62. J. Takakusu, *op.cit.*, p. 65.

63. For details see B.N. Mishra, *op.cit.*, Vol. I, p. 242 and foot-note 156 on p. 268.

64. *Ibid.*, p. 243.

65. G. Roerich, *op.cit.*, pp. 94, 97.

66. H.D. Sankalia, *op.cit.*, p. 180.

67. B.N. Mishra, *op.cit.*, Vol. I, pp. 252-53.

68. Rigzin Lundup Lama (trns. in Hindi), *Bharat Mein Baudha Dharam Ka Itihasa*, K.P. Jayaswal Research Institute, Patna, 1971, p. 55. Taranatha, however, says that even after the destruction of the Dharmaganj in fire efforts were made to restore it, several sacred texts were rewritten and restored. He also gives a list of texts destroyed in fire and partly rewritten later on.

69. Hiranand Sastri, *op.cit.*, p. 89. The Ghosrawan stone Inscription of the time of Devapala reads as *"Nalanda paripalanaya niyatah sanghaasthiteryah sthitah...."*

70. *Life*, p. 106.

71. B.N. Mishra, *op.cit.*, Vol. I, p. 237.

72. For details of these seals see Hiranand Sastri, *op.cit.*, pp. 37, 55, 63.

73 *Ibid.*, p. 40.

74. *Ibid.*, p. 39.

75. *Life*, p. 144 For details of the working of clepsydrae, see, B.N. Mishra, *op.cit.*, Vol. I, p. 254.

76. K.K. Thapalayal, *Studies in Ancient Indian Seals*, Lucknow, 1972, pp. 17-18. For details of these seals see, Hiranand Sastri, *op.cit.* Attempts have been made to locate and identify the villages mentioned in seals with modern villages. For details, see, B.N. Mishra, *op.cit.*, pp. 238-239.

77. Sujata Sinha, *op.cit.*, p. 116.

78. *Life*, pp. 112, 121.

79. For details, see, J. Takakusu, *op.cit.*, pp. 169-79.

80. Hiranand Sastri, *op.cit.,* p. 34.
81. For a good account of Buddhist literature taught at Nalanda, see, B.N. Mishra, *op.cit.,* Vol. I, pp. 244-250.
82. H.D. Sankalia, *op.cit.,* pp. 121-122.
83. *A Study of Indo-Arayan Civilisations,* p. 141 cited in H.D. Sankalia, *op.cit.,* p. 98.
84. *Life,* p. 111.
85. B.N. Mishra, *op.cit.,* Vol. I., p. 251.
86. A. Ghosh, *op.cit.,* p. 39.
87. *Ibid.,* pp. 31-32. See also *ASIR,* 1936-37, p. 44. It is probable that two sets of double ovens discovered from Monastery site 6 also might have been used as furnace.
88. Hirananda Sastri, *op.cit.,* p. 86.
89. *Comprehensive History of Bihar,* Vol. I, Part II, p. 503. See also Hiranand Sastri, *op.cit.,* p. 119.
90. B.N. Mishra, *op.cit.,* Vol. 3, pp. 327-28.
91. For a good account of the art and iconography of Nalanda see, B.N. Mishra, *op.cit.,* Vols. 2, 3; A. Ghosh, *op.cit.,* pp. 37-50. Several other works have appeared on sculptures and bronze images of Nalanda.
92. H.D. Sankalia, *op.cit.,* p. 172, fn. 2.
93. B.N. Mishra, *op.cit.,* p. 257.
94. S. Beal, *op.cit.,* p. 170.
95. *Life,* p. 112.
96. H.D. Sankalia, *op.cit.,* p. 123.
97. B.N. Mishra, *op.cit.,* Vol. I, pp. 282-83.
98. H.D. Sankalia, *op.cit.,* p. 125.
99. *Ibid.,* p. 126.
100. *Ibid.*
101. *Ibid.,* pp. 128-129.
102. *Ibid.,* p. 133.
103. *Life,* p. 112. 104. J. Takakusu, *op.cit.,* p. 84.
105. B.N. Mishra, *op.cit.,* Vol. I, p. 290.

106. *Ibid.*

107. For different views on the native place of Santarakshita see, B.N. Mishra, *op.cit.,* Vol. I, p. 292.

108. H.D. Sankalia, *op.cit.,* p. 141.

109. Hiranand Sastri, *op.cit.,* pp. 89-91.

110. H.D. Sankalia, *op.cit.,* p. 147.

111. For details, see, G. Roerich, *op.cit.,* A Good account of the teachers of Nalanda may be found in P.N. Bose, *Indian Teachers of Buddhist Universities,* Madras, 1923, Sukumar Dutt, *Buddhist Monks and Monasteries of India,* 1962.

112. S. Beal, *op.cit.,* Vol. I, p. XX.

113. B.N. Mishra, *op.cit.,* Vol. I, p. 304.

114. *Ibid.,* p. 306.

115. H.D. Sankalia, *op.cit.,* p. 228.

116. For details see, B.N. Mishra, *op.cit.,* pp. 307-308.

117. H.D. Sankalia, *op.cit.,* p. 232.

118. *Ibid.*

119. S. Beal, *op.cit.,* p. 266 and J. Takakusu, *op.cit.,* p. 177. Hsuan Tsang noticed several *Sagharamas* and nearly 6000 priests living in them at Vallabhi. It was a great centre of *Hinayana.*

4

Odantapuri Mahavihara

In the vicinity of Nalanda *Mahavihara* another University Odantapuri *Mahavihara* was established in the Pala period. This University had a shorter life as compared to Nalanda University. It came into existence in the 8th century CE, and was destroyed by the Turkish invaders towards the close of the 12th century. The information about this University is found mainly in Tibetan and Persian literature and epigraphical sources. Though not as important and reputed as Nalanda or Vikramshila Universities, its role in the development of Buddhist studies cannot be overlooked.

IDENTIFICATION AND LOCATION OF THE *MAHAVIHARA*

Odantapuri *Mahavihara*, an important Buddhist educational centre, besides Vajrasana and Nalanda, was situated in the old Magadha region. The place of the monastery has been identified with Biharsharif, the district headquaters of present Nalanda district (formely in Patna district). The place is very close to Nalanda. The place was also known as Uddandapura, Udantapura, Otantpura, Oddanda and Udandapuradesha (Plate 16). Buchanan, on the basis of a local Jain tradition names the town as Bisalapuri or Visalapuri which was founded by king Padmodaya.[1] Colonel Franklin, suggests the name of the ancient town as Visakhapura, after king Visakha of the Ugravamsa dynasty, a contemporary of Maharaja Srenika of Rajgir. Buchanan further suggested that the Fort of Bihar was called as that of Maga Raja or Magahia Raja, meaning thereby king of

Magadha. It was built in 3-4 centuries CE by Andhra kings.[2] From the accounts of Buchanan and Franklin it appears that Udantapura was an old town wherein the famous *Vihara* was established. To the Turkish invaders the town was known as Dandi or Danda Bihar. Beglar relying on local sources suggested that the place was known as Dandapura as it was the centre of *Dandi Sanyasis*.[3] Cunnigham was also of opinion that ancient Udantapura represents the town of modern Biharsharif, named after Shah Shariffudin, famous saint of Bihar. Cunnigham refers to a Chinese chronicle which mentions the town of Danta. This town is apparently Udantapura.[4] There are epigraphical evidence also to suggest that the ancient name of Bihar or Biharsharif was Uddandapura. Thus, the Bihar Brass Image Inscription of the time of Narayanapala, dated in the 54th year of the reign of the Pala king records a benefaction of Ranaka Tharuka, the son of Ucha and resident of Udandapura.[5] Similarly, the Bihar Image Inscriptions of the time of Surpala I belonging to the 2nd year of the reign of Pala king records the consecration of two images of the Buddha on which the inscriptions were engraved, at the Padikraman *Vihara* in Uddandapura by an old Buddhist monk named Purnadasa in the time of the Pala king.[6] Another inscriptional evidence referring to Udantapura has come to light from Gaya. From the Sun Temple Complex at Gaya an inscription on a stone slab fixed on the wall of temple records repair of the temple, in the reign of Firozeshah Tughlaque of Delhi, by Thakkura Kulachandra, Governor of Gaya, belonging to Dakshinagara in Udandapura region.[7] On the basis of this inscription Patil suggests that Uddandapura name existed even in 14th century CE. The Persian chronicles often refer to the region as Udanda Bihar. It appears that when the Turks came to this part of Magadha, the region was full of Buddhist *Viharas*. They, therefore, named it as Bihar. The town of Udandapura itself lost its old name and came to be known as Biharsharif, while other areas retained the name of Bihar which is still prevalent for the modern state of Bihar.

There is no doubt about the fact that Odantapuri *Vihara* was itself situated in the town of ancient Odantapuri, modern

Biharsharif. Scholars are generally unanimous on this point, but the problem is where to locate the remains of the *Vihara* in ancient town of Odantapuri. As the site is fully occupied by medieval buildings including fort and several tombs, regular and systematic excavations could not be conducted. Broadley, however, refers to some Buddhist structures seen by him around 1872. Though no substantive stuructures were noticed by him but he saw huge heaps of bricks, stones and pillars. He identified the hill to the south-west of the town locally known as Pir Pahadi or Bari Pahadi with Indrasila *guha* of the Buddhist tradition, though Cunnigham did not agree with his identification. Broadley, relying on a local tradition suggested that it was the site of a famous Maghaia *sangat* or a Buddhist monastery. He also noticed here remains of *Chaityas*, portions of gateways and a unique Jain (?) image with an inscription of Madanapaladeva on its pedestal.[8] Thus, according to Broadley the ancient *Vihara* of Odantapuri might have been situated on Pir Pahadi or Bari Pahadi (Plate 17). Several other scholars also suggested that the *Mahavihara* was located on a hillock near Biharsharif. The very name of the *Vihara* Udayantapuri, the 'flying city' would suggest that it was situated on a hill and if viewed from the plain area it looked as if a city (*puri*) were flying (*udyanta*) in the sky.[9] Some other scholars locate the monastery at the mound of Biharsharif. Probably the site of the present Nalanda College, Biharsharif represents the ancient site of the monastery.[10] In view of these conflicting opinions we are not in a position to ascertain the exact location of the *Mahavihara* in modern Biharsharif town unless some new archaeological evidence is unearthed.

THE ESTABLISHMENT OF THE *MAHAVIHARA*

It is rather surprising why another *Mahavihara* was established in Odantapuri while Nalanda *Mahavihara* was in a flourishing condition in its close vicinity. No definite answer to this question can be given. Perhaps the founders of the new monastery in their zeal to spread Buddhism established another Buddhist religious and educational centre at Odantapuri. Another reason seems to be that since Nalanda had become world famous institution, there was heavy rush of students and scholars and it might have become difficult to cope with the ever growing number of scholars at Nalanda. Therefore, to lessen the burden on Nalanda and accommodate new comers another Buddhist educational centre was established at Odantapuri. Besides, the geographical location of the place also favoured establishment of a *Mahavihara* at Odantapuri. The place was situated in Magadha region which was the citadel of Buddhism. While Vajrasana and Nalanda were close to hills, Odantapuri was in plain area. It was situated on well established old land-route easily accessible. It lies on the old route between Rajagriha, the ancient capital of Magadha, and the Ganges. This route was used by religious teachers as well as traders and commoners for going to Vaishali and Sravasti from Rajagriha. Above all, the place was associated with the activities of Buddha as was Bodh Gaya and Nalanda. Hence, it possessed hollowed glamour for the Buddhists. Y. Mishra suggests that Uddandapura (later Biharsharif) was actually Ambalatthika lying between Rajagriha, Nalanda, Pataligrama and the Ganges. It was at this place that Buddha stayed during last phase of his life while going from Rajagriha to Vaishali. He further suggests that there is little difference between *latthika* and *danda* and a *lathi* meant for a mango tree *(ambat latthika)* would naturally be long *ut* + *danda* or *Udanta*.[11] Thus, the association of Buddha with the place favoured the establishment of a monastery here. Moreover, even before the establishment of the monastery the place had acquired some importance. The discovery of two inscriptions, inscribed on a fragment of sandstone pillar, from the Fort area of Bihar (Biharsharif) belonging to the time of Gupta kings Kumaragupta and Skandagupta[12] point in this direction. Thus, there was quite favourable condition for establishing a *Mahavihara* at Odantapuri. The *Mahavihara* itself was named after the place.

Different traditions are preserved in the Tibetan accounts regarding the establishment of the Odantapuri *Mahavihara*. The credit for establishing this monastery is given to the Pala king Gopala or Devapala. Buston, Taranatha and Sumpa refer to prevailing legends regarding the establishment of Odantapuri

Mahavihara. Buston in his *History of Buddhism* suggests that the Pala king Dharmapala, son of king Gopala, the founder of the Pala dynastry, having completed his education desired of building a temple and later the magnificient monastery was built at Odantapuri.[13] It may be pointed out that the same legend about the establishment of the Somapura *Vihara* in Varendri is mentioned, though it was founded by Dharmapala. Taranatha in his *History of Buddhism in India* gives a curious legend about the establishment of Odantapuri *Vihara*. He says that Gopala in the later part of his reign captured Magadha and got constructed a *Vihara* near Odantapuri, named Nalanda. At another place he says that during the time of Gopala or Devapala Sri Odantapuri *Vihara* was also constructed. At that time there lived a *Tirthika yogi* Narada. He needed the assitance of a man who could help him in his *Vetala-Sidhi*. He found a Buddhist *upasaka* named Udaya Upasaka. He received abundant gold from *vetala* and the supernatural power from the *yogi* of flying in the sky. Endowed with this power he flew in sky, reached Sumeru, circled it with its four *dvipas* and came back on earth. With the help of the gold received from *Vetala*, Udaya Upasaka got constructed the *Vihara* of Odantapuri on the model of Sumeru. Udaaya Upasaka did not receive any financial help either from the king or his minsiters but met the expenses of the cosntruction of its monastery by sale of gold received from *vetala*. As long as he was alive he himself managed the affairs of the monastery. However, at the time of his death Udaya Upasaka entrusted this monastery to Devapala.[14] More or less a similar story is given by Sumpa in his *Pag-sam-jon-zang*. He says that a *Tantric* between Gopala and Devapala who wanted to perform a ritual with a corpse to attain the *siddhi* of sword with the gold of which a corpse was converted to enable the *tantric yogi* to perform his ritual to attain the *siddhi*, met Unna who built Odantapuri near Nalanda on the model of Sumeru with its four *dvipas*.[15]

These legends do not give credit to any Pala king for the construction of Odantapuri *Vihara*, but their reliability is doubtful. Much reliance has been put on these accounts by Y. Mishra to suggest that Odantapuri *Vihara* was not constructed by any Pala king. He intends to suggest that the *Vihara* was built by Buddhists with the financial help received from the 'Brahamanical Hindus.'[16] The inaccuracy of the Tibetan accounts become evident from the fact that neither Buston, Taranatha nor Sumpa refer to Dharmapala between Gopala and Devapala. Moreover, Taranatha himself at one place says that Gopala got constructed a *Vihara* named Nalanda (Narendra) near Odantapuri. We all know that Nalanda had earlier origin and from time-to-time several monasteries were added to it. Therefore, there is no truth in the fact that Gopala built Nalanda monastery. Taranatha seems to be confused somewhat. The monastery built by Gopala near Odantapuri (place) might have been named as Nalanda due to its fame. It is also possible that the monastery built by Gopala might have been known as King's Monastery (Narendra) as we know that Vikramshila *Mahavihara* was also known as Rajagriha or Royal *Vihara*. So, if viewd in correct perspective it would appear that Odantapuri *Vihara* was actually built by Gopala. Having conquered Magadha, to establish his fame and reputation, Gopala founded the monastery. Here, we fully agree with S. Dutta and F.E. Keay.[17] Following in the foot-steps of Gopala, Dharmapala got constructed the *Mahaviharas* of Vikramshila and Somapura.

Another objection regarding the credit given to Gopala for constructing Odantapuri *Vihara* is its date. Gopala is said to have ruled between 750-780 CE.[18] The Tibetan accounts suggest that Santarakshita or Santirakshita (705-762 CE) visited Tibet on the invitation of king Khir-son den-stan in 743 CE, stayed there for some time and went to Nepal. He again returned to Tibet and errected the monastery of Sam-ye along with Padmasambha. Santarakshita became the abbot of this monastery, spent his life there and expired in 762 CE. The date of the foundation of this monastery is given as 749 CE. The most interesting part of this account is that it says that the Sam-ye monastery was built on the model of Odantapuri *Vihara* (Plate 18). This statement poses a problem in determining the date of Odantapuri *Vihara* in the time of Gopala as his accepted date is 750 CE. Relying mainly on this statement the probable date of the foundation of

Odantapuri *Vihara* has been fixed at 725 CE, obviously a pre-Pala date.[19] This date has been fixed on presumption that when the Tibetan monastery was built in 749 CE, nearly twenty-five years had passed between the foundation of Odantapuri *Vihara* and Sam-ye *Vihara*. During this period Odantapuri *Vihara* might have acquired sufficient fame and glory so that Santarakshita got constructed Sam-ye *Vihara* on the model of Odantapuri *Vihara*. All these arguments are hypothetical and presumptive. This much is certain that Odantapuri *Vihara* was built after the visits of Hsuan Tsang and I-Tsing in 7th century CE. There might have existed a small and insignificant *Vihara* at Odantapuri before the Palas established their hold over Magadha. The founder of the Pala rule Gopala might have reconstructed or enlarged this monastery or built altogether a new monastery at Odantapuri towards the later part of his rule. The statement that the Sam-ye *Vihara* was built on the model of Odantapuri is obviously late and given in order to enhance the glory of the Tibetan monastery. We have already noticed Taranatha's statement that Odantapuri *Vihara* was built on the model of Sumeru and four *dvipas*. Such statements are hyperbolic and do not deserve serious consideration. The fact remains that Odantapuri *Vihara* was built during the time of Gopala and survived till the end of the Pala period.

HISTORY OF ODANTAPURI

We do not have detailed information about the history of Odantapuri *Mahavihara*. Few inscriptions, mentioned earlier, have come to light from Bihar (Sharif). Some of them belong to the Pala and Gurjara Pratihara dynasties (Surapaladeva, Narayanapaladeva, Madanpala and Mahendrapaladeva) while the rest belong to the reigns of Sultans of Delhi and Mughal emperor Shah Alam II.[20] The literary sources are also silent on the subject. However, it appears that after its establishment in the later part of the 8th century it received patronage of the Pala kings as did other contemporary *Mahaviharas* like Nalanda, Vikramshila, Somapura and Jagaddal. When the Turkish raids on Bihar began towards the close of the 12th

century CE, Odantapuri *Vihara* witnessed rapid decline till its final destruction.

CURRICULUM AND TEACHING

The Tibetan sources, except mentioning names of some teachers/scholars of Odantapuri *Vihara* practically say nothing about the subjects of study and the method of teaching, number of teachers and students there, though the *Blue Annals* (Part II, p. 1031) suggests that twelve thousand Buddhist monks lived there permanently. Taranatha, (*op.cit.*, p. 131), however, says that one thousand monks lived permanently at Odantapuri. Sometimes twelve thousand *bhikshus* congregated there. It may be presumed that as other contemporary universities were centres of *Mahayana* Buddhism, so was the case with Odantapuri *Vihara* also, though to Taranatha *Hinayanists* also lived there. *Mahayana* Buddhism, with its special feature of *Tantrayana* seems to be the chief subject of study. Besides, Sanskrit, logic and philosophy also must have formed part of the curriculum. All scholars related with Odantapuri were reputed persons in logic and *Tantric* studies. An important academic contribution of this monastery was that it developed its own alphabet. Not being satisfied with the use of *Sidhamatrika* alphabet of Uttarapatha and Madhyadesha or Aryavarta and the *Gaudi* alphabet current in Purvadesha, they developed their own *Bhaikshuki* alphabet. While referring to the alphabets used by the Hindus, Alberuni mentions about this alphabet which was used at Udandapura or Udatapura in Purvadesha (eastern country). The use of this alphabet distinguishes Odantapuri from three other universities of early medieval Bihar in the sphere of writing.[21] Much writing work was undertaken at the monastery and several volumes of original texts (manuscripts) were produced. Like other universities, copying of manuscripts also formed part of the activity of monks and scholars. Odantapuri was also a centre of Tibetan translations. Several original volumes were translated here into Tibetan. It appears that the traditional method of teaching in Buddhist *Viharas*, i.e., lecturing the students and tutorial system also prevailed here.

MANAGEMENT OF THE *VIHARA*

Unlike Nalanda, no seal or inscription referring to the management of Odantapuri *Vihara* has come to light as yet. However, we may presume that the affairs of this monastery also might have been managed on pattern of other monasteries. There must have been a chief abbot and other priests to assist him in the management of the *Vihara*. There might have been two categories of managerial staff — (i) administrative staff and (ii) academic staff. There might have also been a *Bhikshu Mahasamgha* at Odantapuri for over all supervision of the *Vihara*. The *Vihara* probably thrived on the financial support received from the Pala kings and local feudatories but we have not come across any land grant in favour of this monastery. Perhaps local people supplied daily needs of the teachers and students of this *Mahavihara*. Some financial assistance might have been provided by the Tibetans also. The University might have sound financial condition. Otherwise it would have been difficult to run the University for nearly four centuries. Unfortunately we do not have any Tibetan account like Chinese of Hsuan Tsang or I Tsing which could enlighten us on different aspects of this famous University.

SCHOLARS/TEACHERS OF THE UNIVERSITY

From Tibetan sources we come to know about some luminaries of Odantapuri *Mahavihara*. Though as compared to the teachers and scholars of Nalanda and Vikramshila *Mahaviharas*, their number is less, but not eminence. Some of the eminent scholars of Odantapuri were Santarakshita, Silarakshita and Dipankarasrijnan Atisa. Besides, out of traditional 84 *Siddhas*, two of them, Yoga-pa and Santi-pa were also associated with this University.

Santarakshita : He was also known as Santirakshita or Dharmashantighosha according to Taranatha. He has been designated as *Mahapandita*.[22] It was he who, along with Padmasambhava, his contemporary, and his own disciple Kamalasila, laid the foundation of the Sam-ye *Vihara* in Tibet. It was he who introduced Buddhist monasticism in Tibet. He was a great *Tantric (Vajrayanist)* scholar. He also became the High Priest of Nalanda and first Head of the Tibetan monastery. He conducted the affairs of the Tibetan monastery for nearly thireen years and expired in Tibet itself. Santirakshita is credited with having written several works on *Vajrayana*, the most important being the *Tattvasidhi*. He also translated many Sanskrit texts into Tibetan.

Silarakshita : Another great scholar of the *Mahavihara* was *Acarya* Silarakshita. It was from *Mahasanghika* Silarakshita that Dipankarasrijnan at the early age of nineteen took the sacred vows at Odantapuri *Mahavihara.*[23]

Dipankarasrijnan Atisa : The most renowned teacher associated with the University of Odantapuri (also with Nalanda and Vikramshila) was Dipankarasrijnan Atisa. He was born in 980 CE and was son of king Kaylansri and queen Prabhavati of Gaur. He either belonged to Bengal or Sahor in Bhagalpur. He was named as Dipankarsrijnan by Silarakshita. The title of *Atisa* was bestowed upon him by the Tibetans. His initiation took place at Odantapuri. He first studied at Vikramshila University and later on moved to Nalanda. After a year's study at Nalanda he went to Maitripada Advayavajra or Avadhutipa and studied the teachings of the *Siddhas* for nearly six years. He also studied at Vajrasana (Bodh Gaya) and went to Suvarnadvipa for further studies. On his return to India via Ceylon, he became the chief priest of both Vikramshila and Odantapuri *Mahaviharas*. He is said to have mediated between the Pala king Nayapala and Kalchuri king Karna. Atisa went to Tibet in 1040 CE, lived there for thirteen years preaching Buddha's gospel. He expired at Nethan near Lhasa in Tibet in 1053 CE at the age of 73. Atisa was a prolific writer. He is said to have written about two hundred books many of them dealing with *Tantra* and translated several Sanskrit works into Tibetan.[24]

Two other renowened scholars of Odantapuri were Yoga-pa and Santi-pa, the famous *Siddhas*. Renowned *Tantric* scholars like Tilopa and Naropa had also connection with Odantapuri.

Yoga-pa : He is mentioned as the 53rd *Siddha.* He lived in Odantapuri and belonged to low caste. His *guru* was Sabra-pa. Taranatha places him during the reign of Mahapala, son of Mahipala, but he was a disciple of Sarha, the *Adi Siddha* and the *guru* of Lui-pa. Thus, he becomes an earlier personality because both Saraha and Lui-pa are believed to have flourished during the reign of king Dharmapala.[25]

Santi-pa : He was one of the *Siddhas* and was also known as Ratnakarasanti. He was born in Magadha in a brahamana family. He had his education at Odantapuri and was ordained in *Sravastivada* sect there. He studied *Sutras* and *Tantras* at Vikramshila with Jetari. He was the teacher of Dipankarasrijnan Atisa and preceptor (*rajacarya mahapandit*) of king Mahipala 1.[26] He was also appointed as the Gatekeeper *Pandit* of the eastern gate of Vikramshila University. Several important works are assigned to him. Some of these were *Prajnaparamitabhavanopadesa* and *Prajnaparamitamitopadesa.* He also went to Ceylon on inviation.

Thus, Odantapuri *Mahavihara* also contributed immensely in the spread of *Mahayana-Vajrayana.* It remained a centre of higher Buddhist learning and maintained close contact with other contemporary Universities. Unfortunately, this University of early medieval India also fell prey to the Turkish invaders. It was destroyed so badly that remains of this University are almost negligible.

REFERENCES

1. Cited in D.R. Patil, *Antiquarian Remains in Bihar,* p.44.
2. *Ibid.*
3. *Archaeological Survey of India Reports,* Vol. VIII, p. 25 *Ibid.,* Vol. VI, p. 191.
4. *Ibid.,* Vol. VI, p. 191.

   Cunnigham was also inclined to identify Yasovarmmapura mentioned in Ghosrawan village and A.C. Banerjee with town of Srinagara mentioned in Nalanda seals. See, Patil, *op.cit.,* p. 44.

5. Bhagwant Sahai, *The Inscriptions of Bihar*, Delhi, 1983, p. 81.
6. *Ibid.*, p. 78.
7. Cited in D.R. Patil, *op.cit.*, 141.
8. For details see D.R. Patil, *op.cit.*, p. 47. However, Patil on another place (p. 54) suggests that this inscription was inscribed on the image of goddess Parvati.
9. Yogendra Mishra, "The University of Odantapuri", *The Journal of the Bihar History Congess (JBHC)*, No. 1, 2008, p. 27.
10. It has also been suggested that the name Odantapuri is derived from its geographical location. A stream of river Panchane was situated in the Western-Southern part of the city. In Pali language the term *Udaka* means river. Thus, as the town was situated at the end of *Udaka* it came to be known as Odantapuri. For details see, Rajiva Ranjan, "Odantapuri Ki Khoj Mein", R. Panth (ed.), *Nalanda Buddhism and the World*, Nava Nalanda Mahavihara, 2001, p. 297.
11. *J.B.H.C.*, p. 27.
12. D.R. Patil, *op.cit.*, p. 46.
13. Buston, *A History of Buddhism* (trns.) E. Obermiller, Part II, p. 157.
14. Rigzin Lundup Lama (trns.), *Lama Taranath's Bharat Mein Bauddha Dharma Ka Itihasa* (in Hindi), Patna, 1971, pp. 109-11.
15. Sumpa, *Pag-sam-jon-zang* (ed.) S.C. Das, Calcutta, 1908, p. cxiii and iii.
16. *J.B.H.C.*, p. 29. Similar view is expressed by Rajiva Ranjan also, See, *op.cit.*, pp. 298-99.
17. For details see, S. Datta, *The Buddhist Monks and Monasteries of India : Their History and Their Contribution to Indian Culture*, p. 354; F.E. Keay, *Ancient Indian Education*, p. 106.
18. B.P. Sinha (ed.) *The Comprehensive History of Bihar*, Vol. I, pt. II, p. 247.
19. *J.B.H.C.*, *op.cit.*, p. 29. It has also been suggested that Odantapuri *Vihara* was built sometimes between 715-725 CE. See, Rajiva Ranjan, *op.cit.*, p. 300.
20. The Pala and Gurjara-Pratihara inscriptions do not throw any light on the history of Odantapuri except recording installation

of images. For details see, D.R. Patil, *op.cit.*, pp. 54-55, B. Sahai, *op.cit.*, pp. 78-81.

21. *J.B.H.C.*, *op.cit.*, p. 30 and foot-note 27, p. 42.
22. Rigzin Lundup Lama, *op.cit.*, p. 113.
23. *J.B.H.C.*, p. 30.
24. For details of Atisa, see, Alka Chattopadhyaya, *Atisa and Tibet*, Calcutta, 1967.
25. *J.B.H.C.*, *op.cit.*, p. 29.
26. S.C. Vidyabhushan, *History of Indian Logic*, Calcutta, 1921, p. 140.

5

Vikramshila Mahavihara

Vikramshila was another important *Mahavihara* of Bihar. It was famous for *Tantric* studies. It was the only *Mahavihara* situated on a river bank. The *Mahavihara* was established in the Pala period and continued to exist for nearly four centuries. Information about this Buddhist educational centre is derived mainly from the Tibetan sources. Much controversy prevailed regarding the exact location of this *Mahavihara* but the latest archaeological excavations conducted by the Archaeological Survey of India has located the site of this world famous University at Antichak, near Kahalgaon in Bhagalpur.

LOCATION OF VIKRAMSHILA

The exact location of the site of Vikramshila *Mahavihara* has been a matter of controversy for long period. Different places were identified with this monastery. Some scholars suggested that Vikrampura in Bangaldesh should be taken to represent the site of the ancient University. However, as the Tibetan texts indicate a close relationship between Nalanda and Odantapuri *Mahaviharas*, both in modern Nalanda district, on the one hand and Vikramshila University on the other, the exact location of the site should be looked in Bihar.[1] A mound located by Buchanan at village Antichak near Bhagalpur, was taken by Oldham to represent the site of Vikramshila *Mahavihara*. "He was so near the truth but his suggestion was ignored by scholars."[2] Alexander Cunningham located the site of the University with village Silao near Nalanda.[3] However, the absence of river Ganga near village Silao does not support this identification as the Tibetan sources explicitly mention that the *Mahavihara* was situated close to the river Ganga. Banerji Sastri suggested that the site of this famous University be located at village Keur, near Hulasaganj in Nalanda district. He based his arguments on the topographical situation and archaeological findings.[4] Here also the absence of river Ganga becomes the greatest hurdle in accepting Keur as the probable site of the ancient *Mahavihara*.

Taking river Ganga as the starting point of the identification of the site of Vikramshila *Mahavihara*, many scholars have tried to locate it in Bhagalpur area, the ancient Anga region. R.L. Mitra suggested that Sultanganj was the probable site of Vikramshila *Mahavihara*.[5] Similar views were expressed by S.C. Das, Rahul Sankrtyayana and some other scholars also tried to locate it near Sultanganj in Bhagalpur, though Rahul Sankrtyayana expressed the view that it might have been situated east of Sultanganj.[6] He was also of opinion that all the sites, right from Shahkund and Sultanganj to Pathargata, should be examined and studied for finding out the truth.[7] N.L. Dey suggested that Patharghata near Colgong (Kahalgaon near Bhagalpur) was the most probable site of the Vikramshila *Mahavihara*. This place was situated on the right bank of the Ganges.[8] The same view was expressed by S.C. Vidyabhushan and some other scholars. R.K. Chaudhary opined that the University lay within Patharghata-Antichak region of the district of Bhagalpur. To quote him, "What seems plausible.... that in the beginning the University had its birth in the Patharghata region and gradually it spread into a bigger area having a host of buildings constructed in course of four centuries."[9] Scholars like B.C. Law and N.P. Chakravarty were also of the opinion that Vateshwara in Patharghata region represents the site of the ancient *Mahavihara*.

The real difficulty in identifying the location of the University is the absence of any seal or inscription bearing the name Vikramshila. However, on the basis of the close examination of the account given in Tibetan sources and recent archaeological findings, the opinion is gaining ground that remains of Antichak represent the actual site of the famous University. Two local intellectuals, L.K. Mishra and Nishikanta Mishra, thoroughly explored the area lying between Patharghata and Antichak and arrived at the conclusion that the architectural remains of village Antichak actually represent the site of the University of Vikramshila.[10] Perhaps taking cue from these and earlier explorations in the area, relevant literary texts and geographical surroundings, B.P. Sinha arrived at the conclusion that village Antichak (Lat. 25.15″ N Long 87.25″ E), about 6 miles from Kahalgaon Railway Station in Bhagalpur district, was the most probable site of Vikramshila *Mahavihara*. To confirm his conclusion, the Department of Ancient Indian History and Archaeology, under the supervision of Professor B.P. Sinha conducted excavations at Dharohara or Dharhara mound at Antichak between 1960-69. During course of these excavations remains of a massive *chaitya* shrine with shrine chambers at four cardinal points were exposed. The plan of the structure was somewhat similar to the one at Paharpur. Antichak site enjoyed a distinct advantage over Sultanganj and Patharghata, in as much as the archaeological remains, as revealed through explorations and excavations are mainly of one cultural period between the late 8th century and the end of the 12th century CE. By implication it meant that the *Mahavihara* was established in a new area, which was not inhabited earlier. In terms of this implication the Antichak site provides a better answer by virtue of it being primarily a Pala site in comparison to Sultanganj where there is a continuous sequence of ancient remains beginning from the Mauryan to the Pala period.[11] The excavators of Antichak site were of the opinion that the massive Buddhist *chaitya* with its distinct mode of construction, the remains of monastic cells and the Buddhist figures discovered from the site, could not but have formed part of the monastic establishment of Vikramshila *Mahavihara*. The long inscription referring to the *Chaitya Dvyam*, the *Vihara* built by Rajyapala (ruler) and the *Kirti* installed by Sahura in the monastery provide further circumstantial evidence to support the contention that Antichak actually represents the site of Vikramshila *Mahavihara*, although the conclusive evidence in the form of seal or sealing bearing the word Vikramshila is still lacking.[12]

After B.P. Sinha, B.S. Verma of the Archaeological Survey of India carried out horizontal excavation at Antichak under the Vikramshila Excavation Project between 1971-1981. During the excavations entire plan of the monastic complex consisting of the central shrine, nearly 208 monastic cells, and other architectural remains, were exposed. On the basis of his findings Verma came to the conclusion that the monastic complex at Antichak belonged to Vikramshila *Mahavihara*. He also expressed the opinion that there is every possibility that the foundation of this *Mahavihara* was laid on the top of the hillock but with the expansion of the *Mahavihara* in course of time the entire activities of the *Mahavihara* shifted from this area to the present excavated site where the remains of the *Mahavihara* have come to light.[13] Thus, two eminent archaeologists of Bihar, have more or less settled the issue of identification of the site of Vikramshila in favour of Antichak. However, it may be pointed out here that no excavation work has been undertaken by the Archaeological Survey of India after the Vikramshila Project. Further excavation of the site is still desirable to get some inscriptional evidence to settle finally the controversy regarding the location of the site of the famous University of Vikramshila. The excavator (B.S. Verma) himself expressed the view that the "Survey should take up a major excavation to unveil further the remains at both the sites, Patharghata and Dharohar mounds which are very close to the remains of the mahavihara."[14] We fully agree with Verma and hope that in near future the Archaeological Survey of India takes up further excavation at these sites.

NOMENCLATURE OF VIKRAMSHILA

Different legends prevail regarding the establishment of Vikramshila *Mahavihara* and its correct name. Taranatha says that king Dahrmapala got constructed Shri Vikramshila *Vihara* in the northern part of Magadha on a hillock by the side of the bank of river Ganga.[15] Thus, according to Taranatha the name of the *Vihara* built by Dharmapala was 'Vikramshila'. Some modern scholars are inclined to call the *Vihara* as 'Vikramshila'. How and why the *Vihara* was named as Vikramshila or Vikramshil is a matter of conjecture. It may be pointed out here that neither any village named as Vikramshil or Vikramshila exists in the Patharghata-Antichak region nor does it find mention in seals and inscriptions discovered so far from the excavations at Antichak. Moreover, the area where it is believed to have been located (Antichak), does not possess any tradition of even an corrupt form of the name of Vikramshila. No popular folklore or songs maintain any account of it nor has it been preserved as such by the local populace. R.K. Chaudhary, therefore, suggests that the name of the University was Vikramshila, but in popular parlance it might have been known as Vikramshil.[16] Some scholars are inclined to believe that since the *Vihara* was situated on a bluff rocky hill, it came to be known as Vikramshila, but this argument is not convincing as the Tibetan name of the monastery (Nam-gnom-nan tshul) does not convey the meaning of either stone or rock, but actually conveys the sense of a strong moral conduct signified by the Sanskrit word equivalent to *Shil.*[17] Some other scholars like R.C. Majumdar opined that the reference to the *Vihara* as *Srimad Vikramsiladeva Mahavihara* indicates that the monastery was named after the founder of the *Vihara* Dharmapala whose *viruda* was Vikramshil, signifying a man with strong moral conduct.[18] In the *Ramacharita* of Sandhyakar Nandi it is mentioned that the father of prince Harivarsa was Vikramshil whose another name was Dharmapala. The evidence of *Ramacharita* also clearly suggests that the monastery was named after Dharmpala who was also known as Vikramshil. S.C. Das refers to a legend according to which *acarya* Kampilya of Nalanda who had attained *sidhi*, foresaw the establishment of Vikramshila and was later born as Dharmpala who is said to have furnished the *Vihara* with four establishments, each consisting of twenty seven monks belonging to four principal sects of Buddhism.[19] Though R.C. Majumdar gives credit of establishing Vikramshila *Mahavihara* to Devapala (820-853 CE) but majority of the sources suggest that this monastery was got constructed by Dharmpala (780-820 CE).

From the above, it becomes quite, clear that Vikramshila *Mahavihara* was built by Dharmapala and was named after him as Vikramshil. There is no substance in some Tibetan accounts that the *Vihara* was named as Vikramshil as a *Yaksa* named Vikrama was suppressed here. 'Vikramshila' does not in any way signify suppression rather it does indicate *Shil* as 'Vikrama' (Strong) as stone or rock.[20] Thus, it appears that the exact name of the *Vihara* was Vikramshil indicating the meaning of strong character. We may fully agree with Alka Chattopadhyaya that the name Vikramshil did not suggest either the meaning of rock or stone or hill, rather "the name of a Vihara is the idea of strong moral conduct (Sila)..... a name was chosen for the monastery for glorifying it as a centre of strong moral discipline."[21]

Although the name Vikramshila *Mahavihara* was known to the Tibetans some Sanskrit texts like *Sarangharasrota tika* and the *Vrhat Svymibhu Purana* also refer to Vikramshila *Mahavihara.*[22] However, the seals and inscriptions discovered from Antichak do not refer to this name. The stone Votive *Stupa* Inscription discovered merely refers to a *Vihara* or monastery built by the *rajyapala*[23], probably the ruler or king who built this monastery but his name is not given. Are we to suppose, therefore, that the inscription refers to Rajyapala, son of Devapala of the Pala dynasty? It is interesting to note here that two terracotta seals were also discovered by B.S. Verma during his excavations at Antichak. One of the sealings (No. 1512) contains a three line inscription. The first two lines read as *Sri Rajayagrara (ha) Mahavihare.* The second sealing (No. 1876) is also a monastic sealing and has inscription which reads as *Sri mjjaya or (rajjaya) Vihara.*[24] These sealings suggest that Vikramshila *Mahavihara* was also known as *Rajagriha Mahavihara* or royal *Mahavihara* in India.[25] As this *Mahavihara* was established by king Dharmapala it might have been known as *Rajagriha Mahavihara* or Royal Monastery.[26] The site of the *Mahavihara* also might have been known to the local people as Sodhala *matha*. This inference is drawn on the basis of an inscribed fragment of a stone slab. The inscription datable to the 12th century CE refers to Sodhala *matha* (*Sri Sodhilayam mathe (bha)).*[27] Sodhala, a native of Gujarat, who wrote the *Udayasundari Katha*, was contemporary of Dharmpala and calls him as the *Uttarapatha Svami*. Sodhala probably was attached to the court of Dharmapala as a minister, and got constructed this brahmanical *matha*.[28] Hence, the village Antichak and the *Mahavihara* situated there might have been popular as Sodhala *matha* also.

HISTORY OF VIKRAMSHILA *MAHAVIHARA*

The Tibetan sources do not enlighten us much on the history of this famous *Mahavihara*, except mentioning eminent teachers and scholars of the University. Still some information about its history may be derived from Tibetan sources. Thus, Lama Taranatha says that king Dharmapala got constructed Sri Vikramshila *Mahavihara* in the centre of which was a temple as large as the Mahabodhi. Around this temple 53 small temples of *Guhyamantra (Mantrayana)* and 540 ordinary temples were constructed. These were encircled by a boundary wall. There were 108 *Pandits* besides *bali acarya, pratisthan acarya, hawan acarya, mushak rakshaka, devadasa* and manager, total 114 people for whom food and cloth was provided. Every month festival was organised for the *dharmasrotas* and sufficient gifts *(dakshina)* was given to them. The head of this *Vihara* was also the patron of Nalanda.[29] Taranatha also informs us about the patronage accorded to this University by other Pala kings and eminent teachers of the University, relation between Vikramshila, Odantapuri, Nalanda, the *Dwarapandits* of Vikramshila and the Turkish raids on this *Mahavihara*. However, the political account of the Palas given by Taranatha is not very reliable as far as the succession of Pala kings and their chronology is concerned. Still Lama Taranatha's *History of Buddhism* gives important information about Vikramshila *Mahavihara*. This *Vihara* flourished under the patronage of the Pala kings like Dharmapala, Devapala, Mahipal, Rampal, Nayapal and others and was renowned for *Tantric* studies. Whereas Nalanda established close links with China, Vikramshila was more connected with Tibet and Nepal due to spread of *Mahayana-Vajrayana* cults there. Vikramshila like Odantapuri remained in existence for nearly four centuries and was finally destroyed by the Turkish invaders towards the close of the 12th century CE. If we believe Dharmasvamin, the *Mahavihara* was so violently destroyed that no remains of it were left and its stones were thrown into the Ganga. However, the archaeological excavations undertaken at Antichak, the site of the *Mahavihara* belies Dharmasvamin's statement.

THE ARCHITECTURAL REMAINS OF VIKRAMSHILA *MAHAVIHARA*

Interesting evidence on the architecture of this *Mahavihara* has come to light from two successive excavations conducted at Antichak. These reveal the massiveness and grandeur of the monastery. We would like to discuss here briefly the architectural remains of Vikramshila with a view to assess the plan of this *Mahavihara*. Remains of two important architecture, the Buddhist *Stupa* and *Samgharama* were exposed during the excavations of 1960-69. The excavations at Dharohara mound exposed a massive *chaitya* shrine with four shrine chambers at four cardinal points. The plan of the structure was similar to those noticed at Paharpur. Two terraces or circumambulatory paths *(pradakshina path)* were noticed. Entrance to the *Chaitya* was provided at the northern end. The outer walls of terrace II were provided with cornices and niches. The niches were decorated with several terracotta plaques depicting Buddha, Buddhist deities, animals and scenes from daily life. Terracotta plaques were so fixed in the plinth walls that the pilgrims could view it while going round the circumambulatory path. The plaques numbered nearly 250. The four shrine chambers at the four cardinal points were attached to a central massive structure representing the drum of a *stupa*. The *stupa* was of cruciform shape. Each shrine chamber was provided with a *mandapa* or ante-chamber in front of it. Walls of the srhine chamber were also decorated with plaques depicting varieties of scenes. Evidence of staircase, use of wood in structure, weep-holes and stone drain to drain out rain water and brick pillars were also found. The most significant discovery was a 29 line long inscription on a stone votive *stupa* from the south-eastern corner of the lower circumambulatory path. According to B.S. Verma (*Antichak Excavations-2* (1971-1981, p. 9) the inscription was found on a pillar stump. The inscription is datable to the 12th century CE. It speaks of a pitched battle between Sahura, a local ruler and Sonadamna who was sent by the king of Vanga to suppress Sahura. It also records the construction of a *Vihara* built by Rajayapala or ruler. The *Stupa* discovered at Antichak has several new features. According to the excavators, "The Buddhist builders of the stupa borrowed the idea of making shrine chambers and ante-chambers or mandapa from the Hindus for offering worship to Lord Buddha. But what-lends an added significance or importance to the above structure is that the shrine chambers and the ante-chambers in four cardinal points are closely interlinked with the drum of the stupa in the centre. Thus, the juxtaposition of the shrine chambers and the ante-chambers in between the drum of the stupa and the circumambulatory path is quite a unique feature, which has not been found elsewhere."[30]

Remains of a monastery or *Samgharama* were also exposed to the north of the Dahrohara mound at Antichak. Remains of floor, verandah on the outerside of the monastery and two rows of rooms on the eastern side of the verandah were exposed. There were altogether four rooms out of which only two were cleared or exposed. All the rooms exposed were characterised by high brick enclosures. Similar constructions were noticed in the south western side of the Dharohara mound. Here also four chambers were exposed. The entrance to the monastery (of the southern wing) was provided at the northern end, indicated by a foot stone found over the floor of the verandah at the northern side. A door opening represented by door frame made of two stone slabs was also found on the northern side. To the south of the stone door frame, a narrow rectangular room and further south of the above room, a row of rooms was noticed. On the whole, the excavations conducted by the team of archaeologists of Patna University brought to light remains of a massive *chaitya* and *stupa*, monastery and monastic cells for the residence of the monks.[31]

Further light on the architectural raims of Vikramshila *Mahavihara* was thrown during the excavations undertaken by the Vikramshila Excavation Project of the Archaeological Survey of India at Antichak. The excavations exposed remains of monastic complex and central shrine. The main entrance to the monastic complex was towards the northern side (Plate 21). Here evidence of flight of steps, *mandapa* or porch, pylons, verandah, courtyard and causeway was found. The most interesting find was the remains of monastic cells, numbering two hundred and fifty-three (Plate 22). The cells were of four categories, i.e., General cells, Projected circular cells, Projected Rectangular cells and Basement cells. There were two hundred and eight general cells, surrounded by the central shrine on all the four sides and on plan, they formed a square monastery. Each cell was provided with a door opening into common verandah. There was also possibly provision for windows in cells. Almost all the cells were provided with a bed platform. The circular cells numbered twenty. These were provided with three bed platforms. The rectangular cells numbered sixteen. Besides, a bigger rectangular suit of three cells was also discovered. These were interconnected with their corresponding regular cells. The most interesting feature of the monastic complex was the provision of basement chamber under some of the cells. Their number was eleven. The basement cells could be entered through a manhole like opening.[32] A 16 m. long stone-built covered drain, crossing the entire eastern wing in the north-east corner of the monastic complex was provided to drain out rain water. An interesting feature of this drain is that at the centre it has a sharp curvature of 160°. This enabled the drain to control the very fast flow of water during rainy-season, and also obstructed the peeping off unwanted elements from outside, right into the courtyard of the monastery.[33] The exist to the monastery was provided through the main northern gate, but there were other two exists also. One was the postern gate, measuring 2.65 m. x 3.28 m. wide. The other one was through a basement passage in the southern wing which measured 13.65 m. x 1.24 m. This passage passed beneath the monastic cells. At the time when the monastery lost royal patronage and there was no one to guard this passage it was closed.[34]

Apart from the monastic complex, the remains of the central shrine were also exposed during this excavation. The exposed central shrine was a huge solid square brick pile in the centre of the inner courtyard rising high up above the terraces. It had four ante-chambers on all four cardinal directions and two circumambulatory paths at two levels, including the ground floor. Flights of steps were provided to reach the first circumambulatory path. The basement wall of the first circumambulatory path had many architectural features. The retaining wall of the second circumambulatory path was adorned with terracotta plaques depicting religious as well as secular themes.[35] The first circumambulatory path was connected with the second one and was covered with a roof. According to the excavator, the most interesting feature of the roofed circumambulatory path is the provision for balconies with arched-ceiling in all the four corners of this shrine. These were of entirely different traditions so far known in this region. The striking departure was the accurate spanning. Thus, without any beam, a semi-circular arch, springing from a moulding of two courses of bricks, was found. Evidence of a *mandapa* or a pillared hall, before the northern anti-chamber also came to light. To enter the main shrine, staircase was provided on northern side only. The northern *garbhagrha* was provided with heavy stone door-sills joined by iron dowels. The floor of the *garbhagrha*, plastered in maroon colour was preserved and noticed by the excavator.[36] The excavations also brought to light the remains of a library hall of the *Mahavihara* (Plate 23) and existence of an old fort, probably constructed with the materials robbed from the monastery.[37] These architectural remains are witness to the massiveness of Vikramshila *Mahavihara*.

EDUCATION AT *THE MAHAVIHARA*

Vikramshila was an educational institution of international repute for higher studies. Therefore, rules regarding admission in the University and its administration were meticulously framed. Eminent scholars in different fields, specially *Tantricism* were enrolled on the teaching staff of the University. Strict rules of discipline were followed by students, though cordial relationship existed between teachers and students. On completion of the studies, students were conferred degrees. It is in respect of teachers and mode of teaching that the standard of Vikramshila University is believed to be higher than that of Nalanda and other contemporary universities.[38]

ADMISSION PROCESS

Just like Nalanda University, admission in Vikramshila University was also made on the basis of entrance test conducted by gatekeepers or *Dwarapandits*. These tests were not written but of oral nature, but whereas we have evidence of four *Dwarapandits* in the University of Nalanda, as many as six of them at Vikramshila are mentioned by Lama Taranatha. According to Taranatha, Acarya Ratnakarsantipa managed the eastern gate, Prajnakarmati southern, Vagishwarkirti western and Nagapa (Naropanta) the northern gate. Besides, Ratnavraja was given charge of first central gate while second central gate was managed by Jnanasrimitra.[39] These *Dwarapandits* were scholars of eminence and master of different branches of knowledge. A student had to satisfy these scholars before being admitted to the University. However, it may be pointed out here that only one entrance gate of Vikramshila monastery was exposed during excavations (northern). This has led some scholars to doubt the authenticity of Taranatha's account, but it is possible that some more entrance gates may come to light during future excavations. Moreover, when Nalanda could have four gates there is nothing surprising if there were six gates in Vikramshila *Mahavihara*.

SYLLABUS OF THE UNIVERSITY

The courses of studies did not differ very much from other contemporary Buddhist educational centres. Study of different branches of Buddhism, specially *Tantrayana* and *Vajrayana* were the main subjects of study. Vikramshila was the chief centre for study as well as practice of *Vajrayana*. Occult science, magic, sorcery and *Tantra* was the most important subject of study. Nalanda also became a centre of *Tantric* studies during later part of its history but Vikramshila surpassed Nalanda in the study of *Tantra*. Taranatha informs us about many masters of magic, *mantravajracaryas* and *Tantrics* of Vikramshila. The Central Hall of the University was reserved for the study of the *Prajnaparmitasutras*, an important element in *Mahayana* Buddhism. It was in this branch of learning that Vikramshila made a name in the field of international Buddhism. The University had many great scholars who wrote and compiled books on *Tantra*. Vikramshila was the best institution for the study of *Tantricism*, patronised by the Pala rulers of Bengal and Bihar. Besides, the University also imparted education in several other subjects like Sanskrit, grammar, metaphysics and logic. The study of logic was essential for countering arguments of other Buddhist sects as well as non-Buddhists, specially brahamanical philosophy and religious dogmas. The other important subjects of study were *Hetuvidya, Chikitsavidya, Sabadavidya, Samkhya, Adhyatmavidya* and *Abhidharma*. Perhaps the study of arts and metallurgy was also included in the subject. Although bronzes from Vikramshila are not numerous as compared to Nalanda but terracotta plaques and sculptures have come in good numbers from Antichak excavations. A good number of Buddhist and Brahamanical scluptures were discovered during the course of excavations. Amongst the Buddhist deities mention may be made of Buddha, Lokesvara Maitreya, Manjusri, Marichi, Mahakala, Tara, Jambhala and Avalokitesvara. The Brahmanical deities include Shiva-Parvati, Vishnu, Surya, Ganesha, Kartikeya, Mahisasurmardini, Mansa, Agni, Vayu, Kuber, Kamdeva, Ganga, Yamuna, Bhairava and Narasimha. A blackstone image of standing crowned Buddha is one of the best specimens of stone sculpture from Vikramshila. Many images of Tara have also been found. A bronze statue of Tara had also come to light. The discovery of Brahmanical deities from Antichak is very significant. It suggests that not only Buddhist deities but Brahamanical deities were also worshipped here. It may be taken to suggest cultural assimilation and cordial relations between the Buddhists and non-Buddhists. The study of arts helped in decorating their sacred shrines and production of images in different *mudras* according to *Mahayanist* and *Vajrayanist* canons. Painting and copying of manuscripts formed another important subject of study. Large number of books written and compiled by scholars were copied by the students. Palm leaf manuscripts were painted. These paintings depict a marked *Tantric* influence. Though they are characterised by sensuous elegance, they display a sense of high technical skills and show conspicuous delicacy and charm.[40]

THE TEACHING METHOD

The teaching method followed at Vikramshila *Mahavihara* was very much similar to those prevalent in other Buddhist educational centres. Little desk work was done by students except copying and painting of manuscripts. Class room lectures and more particularly tutorial system prevailed where students discussed their problems with teachers. Debates and discussions formed essential feature of the teaching method. Regular *Shastrarthas* were held from which students benefitted very much. The students were asked to follow strict rules of discipline. They had to show proper behaviour and ettiquate to their teachers, fellow senior and junior students. A student was expected not only to study under his teacher but also serve him in different ways. The Buddhist ideal of a teacher considering a pupil as his son was practised both in letter and spirit at Vikramshila. A teacher and the student were united by mutual reverernce.

THE LIBRARY

The *Mahavihara* possessed a vast and rich library which catered to the academic requirements of teachers and students. It had rich collection of manuscripts on different subjects, especially *Tantra*. As the copying of manuscripts formed an important part of the courses of studies, the number of manuscripts in library went on increasing considerably. Old, damaged and worn out manuscripts were replaced by new ones. The foreign scholars were also supplied with the copies of manuscripts. The Tibetan translation of works prepared at Vikramshila and their preservation in *Tanjur* and *Kanjur* is an evidence of the fact that large number of manuscripts were prepared and preserved carefully in Vikramshila University library. The maintenance of this library involved heavy finance. It was met by liberal grant received from the patrons of the University, specially the Pala kings. The affairs of the library were managed by the Academic Council of the University. Besides, there must have been distinct class of monks to look after the proper functioning of the library. It may be pointed out here that remains of a library hall was exposed at Antichak during the excavations of 1971-1981 (p. 10).

ADMINISTRATION AND OTHER FEATURES OF THE *MAHAVIHARA*

The administration of this renowned *Mahavihara* differed from Nalanda University. Vikramshila was a royal monastery and hence not as autonomous as Nalanda University. The reigning kings of the Pala dynasty exercised considerable influence over it. We do not find any organised body of monks *(bhikshu smagha)* who managed affairs of the University. Instead it appears that the Chief Priest of the monastery, appointed by Pala kings, managed the affairs of the University with the help of other *acaryas* and monks. We are told by Lama Taranatha that Dharmapala, after the establishment of the *Mahavihara* appointed his *guru* Buddhajnapada as the *Vajracarya* (head of the monastery) of Vikramshila. R.K. Chaudhary, however, suggests that the administration of the University was vested in a Council of six *Dwarapandits* presided over by the chief abbot of the University.[41] Still, there must have been large number of managerial staff of different categories to manage the general, academic and financial matters. The number of monks and *Pandits* differed from time to time. According to Taranatha there were 108 *Pandits* in the time of Dahrmapala and 160 *Pandits* and about a thousand monks who resided there permanently. Even five thousand ordained monks assembled there for occasional offerings in the time of Ramapala.[42] It is difficult to state precisely the number of teachers and students of the University of Vikramshila, but it may be presumed safely that the number might have been fairly large due to the reputation of the University. Arrangements for lodging of students was made by the University. In 10th century CE, a new *Sattra* was added to the University by one of the sons of king Sanatana of Varendra, also known by the name of Jetari, an eminent teacher of the University. We do not find mention of any Chinese scholar or student at Vikramshila, but there were good number of Tibetans there. The Tibetan sources suggest that kings of Tibet got constructed hostels for the residence of Tibetan monks near the main entrance of the monastery of Vikramshila. Bromton, a Tibetan monk and contemporary of Atisa, in his work *Life of Atisa*, mentions a story how a delegation of Tibetan monks after reaching Vikramshila *Mahavihara* in night had to stay in a guest house outside the *Vihara* as the gates of the monastery were closed.[43] This account suggests that for security reasons the gates of the *Vihara* were closed in night. Even in day time, it was not easy to meet eminent Professors of the University without fixing prior appointment. Strict rules regarding meetings and interviews were prescribed and these could not be violated. The monks led a simple life and devoted their time in worship, meditation and studies. But gradually, as the influence of *Tantricism* increased, the solemnity of the *Vihara* became polluted. A class of *Tantrics* known as *Kimsukas* emerged. They indulged in wine and women, magical rites and sorceries, and other attendant vices. Writing condemnatory slogans on the walls, criticising each others on doctrinal matters, and taking recourse to mean things were some of the special features of the *Kimsukas*. Their activity had created a stir on the campus for sometimes.[44]

The Professors of the University were known as *Acaryas* and the head of a monastic establishment as *Adhyaksha*. The *Adhyakshas* and *Dwarapandits* were appointed by kings. The post of *Dwarapandit* was of very high order. The University conferred the degree or diploma of *Pandit* on dislinguished alumni of the

University. This was done by the ruling Pala king. We have the example of Ratnavajra and Jetari who received the degree of *Pandit* from king Mahipala. A religious congregation, resembling modern convocation, was organised wherein the degree was awarded. R.K. Chaudhary, on the basis of a Tibetan account, refers to such a convocation which took place in the time of king Nayapala. To quote him, "In the morning at eight o'clock when the monks congregated together, being conducted by a Sthavira, I was given a seat in the rank of learners. Then first of all, the venerable Vidyakokila came to preside over the assembly. His appearance was noble and majestic. He got exalted and steady like the Sumeru mountain. I asked those near me if he was not lord Atisa. 'What do you say, O Tibetan Ayusmat, this is the very revered Lama Vidyakokila, who, being a lineal disciple of Acharya Chandrakirti, has become a saintly sage. Do you not know that he was the teacher of Atisa.' Then again pointing to another Acarya who was seated at the head of a row, I enquired if he was not Atisa, I was told that he was venerable Naropanta, who, for scholarship in sacred literature, had no equal among the Buddhists. He too was Atisa's teacher. Another Pandita came in grave and solemn mood moving lowly. The king also rose from his seat to do him honour.... Thinking that he must be Atisa himself, I wished to know who he was. I was told that he was Viravajra.... when I interrogated how learned he was, they said they were not aware of the extent of his attainments. When all the rows of seats were filled up, then came Lord Atisa, the venerable of venerables, in all his glory.... There was brightness mixed with simplicity of expression on his face which acted as a magic spell upon those who beheld him."[45]

As in Nalanda free boarding and lodging facilities were provided to students and scholars so that they could fully devote their time and energy in persuit of knowledge. The University received liberal endowments from kings, other feudal chiefs, merchants and devotees of Buddhism to run smoothly the large establishment of the *Mahavihara*. Great stress was put on the attainment of *Shil*. The galaxy of eminent scholars associated with the University like Tilopa, Naropa, Maripa, Atisa etc.

enhanced its prestige in the academic world. The teachers of the University enjoyed more reverence even than kings. The Tibetan sources suggest that when the Raja, possibly Nayapala, came to take his exalted seat in the religious gathering, none of the members, old or young, rose from their seat to mark his arrival. But whenever any scholar came, the *Ayusmatas* rose from their seat to do him honour and mark his arrival. Even the Raja had to rise from his seat to do him honour whenever a scholar came. The students of the University were also highly respected in India and abroad and in matters of royal appointments they got preference over others. The respect and eminence enjoyed by the scholars of this University becomes clear from the fact that the entrance wall of the University was decorated with the portraits of eminent scholars like Nagarjuna, Atisa, many former *Pandits* of the University and even the drawings of many *Siddhas*. Out of 84 *Siddhas* many like Tilopa, Naropa, Sarhapa, Maripa, Santipa etc. belonged to this famous University. These *Siddhas* preached their philosophy in the language of the masses and thus became precursors of the modern eastern vernacular *Maithili*. They wrote many songs to popularise their ideas. Several such songs form part of the *Dohakosa* of Rahul Sankrityayana. The cultural atmosphere of the *Sidhacarya Padas* finds its eloquent expression in the *Varnatnakara* of Jyotirswara Thakur.[46] The University maintained close contact with other contemporary Universities like Nalanda, Vikramshila, Vajrasana and Somapura. Academic relationship also developed between Tibet, Nepal and Ceylon through Vikramshila *Mahavihara*.

EMINENT SCHOLARS OF THE *MAHAVIHARA*

The Tibetan accounts give detailed information about the teachers of Vikramshila University. Lama Taranatha gives names of twelve *Tantric Acaryas* and six *Dwarapandits* of Vikramshila. The *Acaryas* were:

- (i) Jananpada
- (ii) Dipamkara-bhadra
- (iii) Lanka jayabhadra

(iv) Sridhara
(v) Bhavabhadra
(vi) Bhabyakirti
(vii) Leelavajra
(viii) Durjayachandra
(ix) Samayavajra
(x) Tathagatarakshita
(xi) Bodhibhadra and
(xii) Kamalarakshita.[47]

We have already mentioned earlier names of six *Dwarapandits*. Taranatha also mentions names of Haribhadra, Buddhajnanpada, Prashantamitra, Rahulbhadra, Buddhaguhaya, Buddhashanti, Anandagarbha, Jetari, Pragyarakshita, Dipankarasrijnan (Atisa), Abhyajnangupta, Subhakargupta, Sakayasribhadra, Ratnarakshita, Kamalarakshita and others.[48] In between Budhajnanpada, the first abbot and Sakayasribhadra, the last abbot of Vikramshila *Mahavihara*, many distinguished scholars remained associated with this famous University. We would like to discuss here life and works of only some of the eminent scholars of this University.

Budhajnanpada : Buddhajnapada is believed to be *guru* of Dharmapala. He was the first head of the monastery *(Vajracarya)*, appointed by king Dharmapala. In this capacity he continued for a long period. He was also associated with Nalanda University for some time. Taranatha praises his efforts in the spread of *Prajaparamita* and *Sriguhayasamaja* as well as his generosity. It is said that when the *Saindhavasravakas* of Ceylon created trouble, destroyed the silver image of Heruka at Vajrasana and caused stir at Odantapuri and Vikramshila, king Dharmpala took action against them but Budhajnanpada, protected them from the wrath of Dharmapala.[49] He lived for more than eighty years and translated many Sanskrit works into Tibetan. His famous disciple was Prashantamitra.

In between Budhajnanpada and six *Dwarapandits* scholars like Dipamkarbhadra, Lankajayabhadra, Sridhara, Bhavabhadra,

Bhabyakirti, Leelavajra, Durjayachandra, Krishnasamayavraja, Tathagataraskshita, Bodhibhadra and Kamalarakshita adorned the University and popularised *Tantric* studies.

SIX DWARAPANDITS

The Tibetan accounts suggest that there were six colleges, apart from the Central Hall, known as House of Science. These colleges dealt with different branches of study managed by six eminent scholars, known as the *Dwarapandits*.

Ratnakarsanti : He was also known as Santipa. He was born in a brahamana family of Magadha. Initially he studied at Odantapuri but later on came to Vikramshila. From there he went to Somapura *Mahavihara* and stayed there for many years. On the invitation of the king of Ceylon he visited Ceylon and preached Buddhist doctrines there. Santipa gained much eminence. Impressed by his eminence and knowledge king Mahipala of the Pala dynasty invited him to return to Vikramshila and appointed him as the *Dwarapandit* of eastern gate. Santipa is reckoned among one of the *Siddhas* and was a great scholar of *Vyakarana* and *Nyaya*. He is said to have defeated the *Tirthika* disputants while he was working as *Dwarapandit* of Vikramshila.

Ratnakarsanti is said to have written many books, some of which are *Prajnaparamita-upadesa, Sukha-Dukha-Dvayaparityaga-dristi* and *Antarvyapi*. He was nick-named as *Kalikalasarvagya*.

Prajnakarmati : He was the southern *Dwarapandit*. He was a great scholar of Nayaya and also a poet. He is said to have defeated many *Tirthikas* in intellectual disputations. He was a great devotee of Manjusri. Several literary works are assigned to him, the most important being the *Mandalabhishekavidhi*.

Vagishwarkirti : Vagishwarkirti was born in a kshatriya family of Varanasi. His original name was Shilakirti but after attaining the *siddhi* of Vagishwar, he came to be known as Mahavagishwar and Vagishwarkirti. He was an expert in *mantras, sutras, vyakarana* and logic. It is said that he prepared such a chemical by the use of which a man could live upto 150 years and old people could again become young. He is said to have established many religious and educational institutions. He was appointed as *Dwarapandit* (western gate) of Vikramshila and also of Nalanda by the king. From Vikramshila he went to Nepal.[50] One of his important books is *Vajrapanisadhana*.

Naropa : One of the greatest scholars of Vikramshila was Naropa (Nadapa). He was a disciple of Shantipa and Tilopa. Many miraculous legends are associated with him in the Tibetan texts. He was born in a royal family of Bengal. His parents were Shantivarman and Srimati. In his early age he went to Kashmir for studies. He spent some time at Phullhari *Vihara* (Puspahari) and then went to Nalanda where he was elected as the gate keeper of the monastery. Later on he became a *Dwarapandit* of Vikramshila also. He wrote many texts on *Guhyasamajatantra*. Naropa is believed to be a scholar of the *Mantrayana* school of thought consisting of *Paramityana* and *Mantrayana*. His moral remains are said to be preserved in Kanishka *Vihara* at Peshwara.

Ratnavraja : Another great scholar of Vikramshila was Ratnavraja, belonging to a learned brahamana family. He studied all *sutras, Mantrayana* and other allied subjects in Kashmir and defeated many *Tirthikas*. In recognition of his scholarship king Mahipala conferred on him the degree of *Pandit* and appointed him as the *Dwarapandit* (first Central gate) of Vikramshila *Mahavihara*. He is said to have written many books, the most important being *Hevajrastrota*.[52]

Jnansrimitra : He was born in Gauda. Earlier he was a renowned scholar of *Tripitaka* of *Saindhava-Sravaka* sect, later on he became an ardent champion of *Mahayana* Buddhism. He made a deep study of *Guhaya mantra* and *Tantras*. He wrote a long series of monographs on controversial subjects, designed to establish the doctrine of Dharmkirti and Prajnakargupta despite all criticisms of Brahamana logicians. Some of his important literary works include *Bhedabhedapariksa, Isvarvada, Yoginirnayaprakarnam* and *Advaitavindupra-karnam*.

OTHER EMINENT SCHOLARS OF THE UNIVERSITY

Apart from the six *Dwarapandits* we come across life and works of many other scholars, *Tantrics* and *siddhas* associated with Vikramshila. Amongst them we would like to mention here briefly about Dipankarasrijna Atisa, Jetari, Abhayankaragupta and Sakyashribhadra.

Dipankarasrijna Atisa : We have already discussed about this scholar in connection with Nalanda, but few more lines may be added about him here. He is regarded as the most shining star of the University of Vikramshila. He was a widely travelled man possessing encyclopedic knowledge. His original name was Chandragarbha. Name Dipankarasrijnan was given to him by his teacher Silarakshita at Odantapuri monastery. The Tibetans called him Atisa. He was appointed as the chief abbot of Vikramshila University, most probably by the Pala king Nayapala. He is said to have mediated between Nayapala and Karna, son of Kalchuri king Gangeyadeva.[53] Under the supervision of Atisa, Vikramshila monastery greatly prospered and its fame spread far and wide. New and large accommodations for the monks were provided and new subjects of study and methods of teaching were introduced. He enforced discipline in the University very strictly and is said to have expelled Maitrigupta, a *Tantric*, for taking wine. While at Vikramshila Atisa had in his charge 18 keys of *Viharas* and temples. Atisa was connected in one way or another with all Buddhist *Viharas* of his time. He went to Tibet on the persuasion and invitation of the Tibetan king. There he cleared Tibetan Buddhism of foreign and heretical elements and started a movement which may be called 'Lamaist Reformation'. The Tibetans greatly revered him and regarded Atisa as incarnation of Manjusri. His name appears in an inscription along with Lama Rin-chen-bsing-lo.[54]

Jetari : He was probably a son of Santan, a petty king of Varendri. He was a student as well as a teacher of Vikramshila University. King Mahipala bestowed upon him the title of *Pandit*. He was a great devotee of Manjusri. He was teacher of

Dipankarasrijnan Atisa. He is credited with having written many texts, some of them are *Hetutattvopadesa, Nairatmyasiddhi* and *Jatinirakarna*.

Abhyankaragupta : He was a great scholar of *Tantra* and contemporary of Pala king Ramapala. Perhaps he was born in a kshatriya family near Deoghar. He was the preceptor of Pala king Ramapala. Abhyankaragupta had the distinction of adorning the post of chief abbot of Vajrasana, Nalanda and Vikramshila. He is said to have written and translated nearly thirty-five books like *Nishpannayogavali*. He also wrote a commentary in eight thousand verses on the *Prajnaparamita*. He was regarded as the *Siddhacarya*.

Sakyasribhadra : Sakyasribhadra had the distinction of being the last abbot of Nalanda. Though born at Parvarapur in Kashmir, he spent long years of his life in Bihar before going to Tibet. He visited Vajrasana, Nalanda, Odatnapuri and settled at Vikramshila. While at Vikramshila he was invited by the Chinese king to come to his country but Sakyasribhadra did not go to China. He had good relation with the Pala kings of Magadha and possibly stayed for some time at Jayanagar, near Lakhisari with Pala king Palapal.[55] Sakyasribhadra was a renowned scholar and prolific writer. Several literary works are credited to him. Some of his famous books are *Mahayanopadesgatha, Manjusrikalachakra* and *Aryatara-sadhana*.

Towards the later period of Sakyasribhadra the political condition in Bihar and Bengal had deteriorated considerably. Turkish raids were taking place frequently. Its impact was felt on educational institutions also. A graphic description of the situation is given by Lama Taranatha.[56] It is said that Sakyasribhadra was asked in dream to leave Vikramshila and move towards east. He, therefore, went to Jagaddala *Mahavihara* in Bengal where he lived for three years,[57] but situation was very bad there also. He, therefore, decided to go to Tibet which was more safe than Bihar and Bengal. By this time (towards the close of 12th century CE) along with Vikramshila, Nalanda and Odantapuri were also facing troubled days. Therefore, a large number of monks from these monasteries, under the leadership of Sakayasri went to Tibet and settled there. He reached Tibet in or about 1204 CE and strengthened *Mahayana* and *Tantric* Buddhism in Tibet. Staying for nearly nine or ten years in Tibet, he returned to his homeland Kashmir where he died at the age of ninety nine years in 1225 or 1226 CE. His materials like *civara* etc. alongwith his image are still preserved in a monastery in Tibet.[58]

Thus, after remaining in existence for nearly four centuries, the University of Vikramshila, like Nalanda and Odantapuri, was lost in pages of history for ever. Much attention has not been paid by historians and scholars to unravel different facades of this world famous University of *Tantra*. It is hoped that more light would be thrown on this University by future researches and archaeological excavations of Antichak, the supposed site of Vikramshila *Mahavihara*.

REFERENCES

1. B.P. Sinha, *Directory of Bihar Archaeology*, p. 1.
2. *Ibid*.
3. Cunnigham, *A.S.I. Report*, VIII, p. 75.
4. *J.B.O.R.S.*, XV, pp. 264-276.
5. *J.A.S.B.*, XXX, p. 360.
6. Rahul Sankrtyayana, *Purattatva Nibandhavali* (in Hindi), p. 274.
7. R.K. Chaudhary, *The University of Vikramshila*, The Bihar Research Society, Patna, p. 3.
8. *J.A.S.B.*, V, pp. 1-19 and Vi, p. 7.
9. R.K. Chaudhary, *op.cit.*, p. 4
10. *J.B.P.P.*, I, p. 192.
11. A.K. Singh and Dilip Kumar, *Antichak Excavations Report (1960-69)*, Department of Ancient Indian History and Archaeology, Patna University, p. 15.
12. *Ibid.*, p. 19.
13. B.S. Verma, *Antichak Excavations-2 (1971-1981)*, Archaeological

Survey of India, New Delhi, 2011, p. 7, 391, cf. R.K. Chaudhary, *op.cit.*, p. 8.

14. *Ibid.*, p. 392.
15. Rigzin Lundup Lama (trns.) *Baudha Dharma ka Itihasa* (in Hindi), p. 116.
16. R.K. Chaudhary, *op.cit.*, p. 12.
17. *Ibid.*, p. 9.
18. For details see, R.C. Majumdar (ed.), *History of Bengal*, Vol. I, p. 115.
19. Cited in R.K. Chaudhary, *op.cit.*, p. 11.
20. *Ibid.*, p. 10.
21. Alka Chattopadhyaya, *Atisa and Tibet*, pp. 105 ff.
22. Cited in *Antichak Excavations Report (1960-69)*, p. 10 cf. also R.K. Chaudhary, *op.cit.*, p. 10. The names used in these texts are *Srimad Vikrama-sila-deva-Vihariye* and *Vikramsilasivihare* respectively.
23. *Antichak Excavations Report (1960-69)*, p. 66. For details of this inscription see, *Ibid.*, pp. 62-66. See also *Antichak Excavations-2 (1971-1981)*, Appendix-III, pp. 427-430.
24. *Antichak Excavations-2 (1971-1981)*, pp. 162, 165.
25. *Ibid.*, p. 13.
26. *Ibid.*
27. *Ibid.*, p. 175. However, Sodhala was name of a person and not place as suggested by the excavator. See p. 175.
28. *Ibid.*, p. 14.
29. Rigzin Lundup Lama, *op.cit.*, p. 116.
30. *Antichak Excavations Report (1960-69)*, p. 37.
31. For details of architecture, see, *Ibid.*, pp. 26-39.
32. For details, see, *Antichak Excavations-2 (1971-1981)*. pp. 77-84.
33. *Ibid.*, p. 85.
34. *Ibid.*, p. 85-86.
35. For details of these plaques, see, *Ibid.*, pp. 213-234 and Appendix II, pp. 397-426: See also R.K. Trivedi, *Terracotta plaques from Archaeological Remains of the Vikramshila Mahavihara at Antichak* in

R. K. Sinha, Om Prakash Pandey (ed.) *Studies in History and Archaeology of Vikramshila Mahavihara: The Last Becon of Buddhist Philosophy*, Varanasi, 2015, pp. 111-119, Umesh Chandra Dwivedi, *Sculptural Art of the Vikramshila Mahavihara, Ibid.*, pp. 87-97.

36. *Ibid.*, pp. 87-88.
37. *Ibid.*, pp. 9-10.
38. R.K. Chaudhary, *op.cit.*, p. 25.
39. Rigzin Lundup Lama, *op.cit.*, pp. 124-128.
40. Kiran Sahaya, *Vikramshila: Itihas Evam Purattatva* (in Hindi), Patna, 1998, p. 15.
41. R.K. Chaudhary, *op.cit.*, p. 24.
42. *Ibid.*, p. 52.
43. Rigzin Lundup Lama, *op.cit.*, pp. 116, 131.
44. Cited in Alka Chattopadhyaya, *op.cit.*, p. 416.
45. R.K. Chaudhary, *op.cit.*, p. 18.
46. *Ibid.*, p. 35.
47. *Ibid.*, pp. 19, 23.
48. Rigzin Lundup Lama, *op.cit.*, p. 3.
49. *Ibid.*, pp. 115-137.
50. *Ibid.*, pp. 117-118.
51. *Ibid.*, pp. 125-126.
52. *Ibid.*, pp. 126-127. See also, R.K. Chaudhary, *op.cit.*, pp. 23, 65-67.
53. *Ibid.*, p. 127, R.K. Chaudhary, *op.cit.*, p. 28.
54. *Ibid.*, pp. 127-128, R.K. Chaudhary, *op.cit.*, p. 28.
55. R.K. Chaudhary, *op.cit.*, p. 47. See also pp. 39-48 and Alka Chattopadhyaya, *op.cit.* for details of Atisa's life and works.
56. *Ibid., op.cit.*, p. 49.
57. Rigzin Lundup Lama, *op.cit.*, pp. 132, 134.
58. *Ibid.*, p. 134.

6

The Decline and Desertion of the Mahaviharas

The *Mahaviharas* of early medieval India went out of existence towards the close of the 12th century or early 13th century CE. Why and how these educational centres came to an end is a matter of great controversy. The Tibetan accounts and many modern scholars suggest that the Turkish invasion or their inroad in Bihar and Bengal caused decline and disappearance of these Buddhist educational centres. However, this may be one of the factors for the decline of the Universities, but there might have been several other causes responsible for the decline of these educational centres.

THE TIBETAN ACCOUNTS ON DECLINE OF THE *MAHAVIHARAS*

We have two important Tibetan sources, *Biography of Dharmasvamin*[1] and *History of Buddhism in India*[2] by Lama Taranatha. Dharmasvamin was a Tibetan monk who visited India between 1234-36 CE. From his account it appears that there was political chaos in Bihar after the Turkish inroad. Despite many difficulties and dangers Dharmasvamin visited places like Vajrasana or Bodh Gaya, Rajagriha, Nalanda and Vaishali. Signs of decay and anarchy could be noticed by him at all these places. Constant raids were being made by the Turushkas (Turks). Dharmasvamin stayed for nearly three months at Vajrasana. The place was deserted and only four monks stayed there. The king of Magadha Budhasena who resided at Vajrasana, had fled to forest due to fear of Turks. Nalanda was in shambles. Most of its *Viharas* were damaged by the Turushkas and there was no one to look after them or make offerings. Only two *Viharas*, Dhana-ba and Ghu na-ba were in a serviceable condition. *Mahapandit* Rahulsribhadra, a ninety year old monk and abbot was residing there with nearly 70 monks. While Dharamasvamin was staying at Nalanda, a message came from Jayadeva, a lay supporter of Rahulsribhadra of Odantapuri, that the Turks were planning to raid Nalanda. Hearing this message, all the monks fled from Nalanda. Only Rahulsribhadra and Dharmasavamin remained there. Dharmasvamin carried his *Guru* on his shoulders and took shelter in a nearby temple of Jinanatha, which had been earlier ravaged by the Turks and stones of temple taken to Odantapuri to construct a mosque there. While they were hiding in this temple, nearly 300 Turkish soldiers raided Nalanda but could not find them. Dharmasvamin does not mention the libraries of Nalanda nor did he get any manuscript copied there. Probably the libraries at Nalanda were completely destroyed by the time of the arrival of Dharmasvamin The fear of Turkish raid loomed large over Vaishali also, an old sacred place for the Buddhists. Dharmasvamin did not go to Odantapuri as the Turks had established their military headquarters and the University might have been destroyed. Dharmasvamin did not go to Virkamshila as well as "there was no trace of it left, the Turuksha soldiery having razed it to the ground, and thrown the foundation stones into the Ganga".[3] The account of Dharmasvamin, thus, clearly suggests that due to Turkish invasions, the *Mahaviharas* of early medieval India, had almost been destroyed completely.

Similar account of the destruction of educational centres of Bihar at the hands of the Turks is given by Lama Taranatha. Much similarity can be noticed in the details given by Dharmasvamin and Lama Taranatha. Taranatha at many places refers to the destruction of *Viharas* by the Turks. At one place he says that the Persian king got destructed Magadha by Turushkas in the time of king Dharmachandra (unidentified). Serious damage was caused to Sri Nalanda also. During the time of Pragyarakshita, a *Pandit* of Virkamshila, the Turks raided Vikramshila but as a result of religious sacrifice performed by Pragyarakshita, the Turks fled away. Many of Turkish soldiers were killed by lightning. Taranatha also refers to Chandra, a Turushka king of Antarvedi, who destroyed Magadha. Both Odantapuri and Vikramshila were destroyed and many monks were killed.[4] Thus, according to Lama Taranatha the Universities of Nalanda, Odantapuri and Vikramshila as well as other educational centres of Magadha region became a victim of Turkish raids and plunder. Another Tibetan work of Sumpa Khanpo Yese Paljor *Pag sam-Jon-Zang* or *History of Buddhism: Its Rise, Decline and Downfall,* on the authority of Kashmiri monk and the last abbot of Virkramshila *Mahavihara*, Sakayasribhadra tells us that the *Viharas* of Odantapuri and Vikramshila were destroyed by the Turks and almost all monks killed.[5] The destruction of the University of Odantapuri by the Turks is confirmed even by the Persian sources. The *Tabaqat-i-Nasiri* of Minhaj-i-Siraj preserves an account of the destruction of Odantapuri. According to Minhaj, Muhammad Bakhtyar Khalji in February 1199 organised an attack upon the fortified city of Bihar with nearly 200 horsemen. He went to the gate of the fort and waged war against unaware enemy. With great valour and audacity he succeeded in capturing the fort. Great booty fell into the hands of the invaders. Most of the inhabitants of the place (or fort?) were Brahamanas with shaven head. They were all slain. Besides a great amount of booty, large number of books also fell in the hands of the invaders. Being unfamiliar with the script or contents of books, the Muhammadans called for some persons to explain the content of these books, but as all men were killed, there was none to explain it. The Muhammadans, then realised that it was not a fort but a place of study, college or *madarsa* or *Vihara*.[6] These sources point out that the destruction of the Universities was caused by violent Turkish raids. Similarly, due to Arab raids the hold of the Maitrakas weakened and Vallabhi University lost the support of its patrons and gradually declined.

ARCHAEOLOGICAL EVIDENCE OF DECLINE OF UNIVERSITIES

Signs of decline were noticed during excavations of Nalanda, Odantapuri and Vikramshila *Mahaviharas*.

Nalanda : Of all the University sites, it was Nalanda only which was extensively excavated. During several excavations of the site it was noticed that the buildings of this University were destroyed by fire. The evidence of burnt wooden pillars and scantlings and beams were found from the monastery site No. 11. "There are abundant signs left in the ruins of burnt wooden beams, doors, images, grains etc. to prove that there was a general outbreak of fire at Nalanda, at least once, from which all the buildings existing at that time suffered more or less. The students and monks must have fled away in panic ...."[7] Interesting evidence of the destruction of structures has also come from an inscription found at the temple site No. 12. The inscription was inscribed on a piece of stone-door-jamb. It records destruction by fire during the time of Mahipala *['Om) Sriman-Mahipala deva-rajya-samvat 11 Agnidah (o) ddhare...].*[8] It also records something saved from fire and a grant made by Baladitya of Telhara near Nalanda. However, the inscription does not tell us either about the cause of fire, the structure destroyed or the name of place where fire broke out. Patil on the basis of this inscription suggests that the temple was restored by Baladitya after its destruction in fire and it would give an impression that the end of Nalanda was fast approaching in the first decade of the 11th century CE.[9]

The cause of fire at Nalanda is not certain. We do not know whether the fire was caused accidently or by ouside agencies. Lama Taranatha gives an account of the destruction of the libraries and manuscripts kept there. According to him a fire caused by the *Tirthikas* destroyed these libraries.[10] However, there is no clear evidence to suggest that the structures and libraries of Nalanda were destroyed by the Turkish invaders though they might have caused damage to these. A possible reason for the recurrent fire at Nalanda is suggested by Patil. As cooking was done inside the monasteries, it must have involved storage of fuel consisting of wood and other combustible material. Moreover, monks might have used naked lamps in night. These might have caused accidental fire and damage to wooden fittings of structures.[11] As wood was used on large scale in the structures of Nalanda, any fire must have caused serious damage to the buildings. However, these fires did not cause total decline and desertion of monasteries. The damaged portions were rebuilt.

It may be mentioned here that from Telhara also, which was very close to Nalanda, a thick layer of ash was found during excavations. It indicates some kind of conflagration at the site.

Odantapuri : No systematic excavation was conducted at Odantapuri. Therefore, archaeological evidence pertaining to the decline of this University is almost negligible. However, several tombs at Biharsharif suggest that they were built mostly out of materials like stone carvings, pillars etc. taken from earlier structures. Remains of Buddhist monastery, basement of a *stupa,* heaps of brick and stones and pillars were found by Broadley and Cunnigham.[12] These suggest destruction of the site of Odantapuri *Mahavihara,* possibly by Bakhtiar Khalji and successive Turkish military commanders who established their permanent administrative centre at Biharsharif and got constructed a fort out of materials of Odantapuri *Mahavihara.*

Vikramshila : The excavations conducted at Antichak by the Department of Ancient Indian History and Archaeology, Patna University and Vikramshila Excavations Project of the Archaeological Survey of India, exposed some archaeological evidence of the destruction of Vikramshila *Mahavihara.* Evidence of partial destruction and additions and repairs were noticed at the *chaitya* shrine. The first phase of destruction has been connected with the pitched battle that took place between the Vanga army led by Sonadamna and the local ruler Sahura who not only defeated Sonadamna but probably succeeded in stopping army from doing further damage to the Buddhist *Chaitya.*[13] Thus, there is evidence to suggest that the *Mahavihara* possibly suffered partial destruction as a result of pitched battle nearby the monastery. Moreover, we have also evidence of fire. Remains of charred wood and trace of conflagration in all the shrine chambers and the ante chambers clearly indicate that the site suffered the second destruction some time after the 12th

century CE during the Muslim period.[14] The second phase of destruction 'may thus be linked to Turushka invaders' who are generally regarded as responsible for the destruction of Vikramshila *Mahavihara*.[15] Similar views are expressed by B.S. Verma also. According to him, "the excavations indicated that a violent destruction robbed the establishment of its grandeur. It is further validated by the remains of the fallen and broken stone-pillars, dis-jointed from their bases, robbed off courses of bricks and extensive deposit of ashy layers found in the excavations. In other words the destruction of the monastery was completed by a planned attack by some outer elements."[16]

The archaeological excavations, thus, hint at some of the possible causes of the decline of the Universities, but these were not the only causes. We have to look for some other causes also for decline and desertion of early medieval Universities of India. It may be pointed out here that the destruction of the *Mahaviharas* of Odantapuri and Vikramshila was sudden and complete but decline set in at Nalanda gradually and it continued to survive for some more years even after the decline and desertion of Odantapuri and Vikramshila.

CAUSES OF THE DECLINE OF THE MAHAVIHARAS

The causes of the decline of the *Mahaviharas* of India were manifold. These included several political, economic and socio-religious causes.

Political Instability

In the post-Harshavardhan period Bihar and Bengal were partitioned amongst small kingdoms. There was no sovereign authority to check and control these warring states. Virtually situation like *matsyanya* prevailed. To end this political anarchy Gopala was elected as the king in Varendri. With Gopala (750-780 CE) was laid the foundations of the Pala empire. Gopala extended his control over Bihar (Magadha) also. The Palas ruled over Bihar and Bengal for nearly four centuries (750-1200 CE). The important kings of the dynasty were Dharmapala, Devapala, Narayanapala, Mahipala I, Ramapala and Govindapala. Some scholars regard Palapal as the last ruler of the Pala dynasty who ruled over Magadha from 1165 to 1199-1200 CE.[17] Under their rule the region prospered and Buddhist monasteries flourished as the Palas were generally champions of Buddhism. The Buddhist educational centres received liberal endowments from them. However, the Palas did not rule uninterruptedly for long period. Soon after the death of Devapala war of succession started in the Pala dynasty. The Pala empire seems to have been divided, at least temporarily, in three independent kingdoms of Anga, Vanga and Magadha. Taking advantage of the situation, parts of Bengal and Bihar were captured by Mahendrapala of the Gurjara-Pratihara dynasty, but Narayanapala restored Pala authority over those areas. Mahipala I seems to be the last great king of the Palas who restored Pala empire to a dignified extent but his power was considerably weakened due to *Kaivarta* revolt of its chief Divya. Mahipala virtually lost Varendri to Divya and even lost his life at the hands of the *Kaivarta* chief. After him the Pala empire began to disintegrate rapidly. During the time of his son Nayapala struggle with Kalchuri king Karna began. Perhaps Karna was defeated in Magadha and peace was made between the Palas and the Kalchuris due to efforts of Dipankarasrijnan Atisa. But this was a temporary truce. Many independent kingdoms arose and the dismemberment of the empire went on. Many feudatories asserted their independence and carved out their own kingdoms. In Gaya region Sudraka became independent. Vanga also became independent while in Anga a Rashtrakuta family under Mathandeva emerged powerful. The Chikora dynasty also emerged in Gaya region. Perhaps, the Pala dominions also suffered due to invansion by the Chalukayan prince Vikramaditya VI. The situation was further aggravated due to war of succession amongst sons of Vigrahpala III (Mahipala II, Surapala II and Ramapala). Ramapala became the last powerful king of the Palas. By this time many independent kingdoms or chiefdoms had emerged. Sandhyakara Nandi in his *Ramacarita* (II, 5, 6 and 8) gives a list of thirteen such chiefs who helped Ramapala in recovering the lost ground and crushed the rebellion of the *Kaivarta* Bhima. Though Ramapala succeeded in restoring the semblence of authority of the Palas but the situation was passing out of his control. He lost Mithila to the Karnatas and faced Gahadavalas also who were trying to penetrate in Pala dominions. The situation completely went out of hand during Ramapala's successors (Kumarpala, Gopala III, Madanapala, Govindapala and Palapala). The Pala empire moved swiftly towards disintegration. The situation was further aggravated by the incursions of the Gahadavalas and the Senas. The Gahadavalas captured large part of South Bihar while the Senas ousted Palas from Bengal and later on Magadha also was wrested by the Senas from the Gahadavalas. The Pala rule was confined to a small territory in Bihar. It has been suggested that Palapala was the last king of the Pala dynasty who ruled over Magadha. It was probably this king, who held the territories stretching along the Ganges from Odantapuri and Nalanda to Vikramshila at the end of the 12th century CE and was defeated by the Turks (Bakhtiyar Khalji), though his name is mentioned neither in the *Tabaqat-i-Nasri* nor in other Persian sources.[18]

The outline of the political condition of Bihar and Bengal under the Palas discussed above, suggests that political chaos and anarchy prevailed towards the later part of the 11th and 12th centuries. It developed an atmosphere of insecurity. In such a situation it was difficult for students and teachers to pursue studies peacefully in the Universities. If we are to believe Lama Taranatha, many scholars and teachers left Vikramshila and Odantapuri *Mahaviharas*, went to Tibet, Nepal, South-West India and even Kamboja.[19] Similar case might have been with Nalanda, Vajrasana and other monastic educational centres due to insecurities. Dharmasvamin clearly mentions how people, and even king of Vajrasana, Nalanda and Vaishali spent their night in perpetual threat of the Turks who had begun their raids by the end of the 12th century. Moreover, the unsettled political situation also affected adversely the economic support to these Universities and they gradually went out of existence.

The Turkish Raids

Some of the Tibetan, Buddhist and Persian sources and

many modern scholars would suggest that the Universities of Bihar were destroyed by the Turkish invaders, particularly Bakhtiyar Khalji. The Turks razed the buildings to the ground, put it on fire, plundered and looted and killed monk residents. The survivors managed to escape and fled away. We have already referred to accounts of Dharmasvamin, Sumpa, Taranatha and Minhaj in this connection. It has been suggested that even before the raids of Bakhtiyar Khalji, the Turks had raided Magadha in the time of *acarya* Lilavarja of Vikramshila. In the time of *acarya* Kamalarakshita also the Turks raided Vikramshila but the soldiers placed there for the protection of the *Vihara* chased and killed many invaders.[20] In fact, even before Bakhtiyar Khalji the Turks were active in western part of Patna (old) district. The Maner copperplate recording grant of villages in the Maniyara (Maner) *pattala* by the Gahadavala king Govindachandra indicates that as early as 1124 CE the people of Maner were subjected to a tax called *Turushkadanda*. This levy was raised either to buy the Turks or for bearing the expenses of defending the Gahadavala kingdom against them.[21] Maner probably served as the military base for the Turks. Moving from Maner Bakhtiyar Khalji captured the town of Bihar (Biharsharif). The University of Odantapuri was completely destroyed. Bihar was made military headquarters for further military raids on Nalanda, Vajrasana and other adjoining areas. After some years, encouraged by recognition of his victories by Qutubuddin Aibak of Delhi and having subjugated the whole of Bihar, Bakhtiyar Khalji moved towards Bengal. He passed through Kiul, Lakhisarai and Bhagalpur and destroyed the University of Vikramshila in or about 1204. Its destruction was total by the time (1234 CE) Dharmasvamin came to India. The Turkish raids caused great damage to the Buddhist educational centres.

The case of Nalanda was somewhat different from Odantapuri and Vikramshila. While the former two went out of existence, Nalanda somehow survived the Turkish raids, though it also faced the brunt of the raids. It is generally believed that in course of the capture of Bihar (Biharsharif) Bakhtiyar Khalji moved towards Nalanda which was just few miles away from

Odantapuri and raided Nalanda also.[22] However, the most surprising thing is that where as Minhaj specifically mentions the invasion and sack of Hisar-i-Bihar and Adwand Bihar, he does not name Nalanda at all. Are we to suppose that Nalanda was included in Hisar-i-Bihar and was not separately mentioned? It was perhaps true, at least from administrative point of view. D.R. Patil advances the argument that by the time of the invasion of Bakhtiyar Khalji in 1197 (or 1199), Nalanda had ceased to be a 'living institution of great repute or importance, at the time of the invasion of Bakhtiyar Khalji in 1197 CE. Quite before Bakhtiyar Khalji's invasion, Nalanda had perhaps fallen to decay or ruins already.'[23] However, the argument of Patil does not seem to be convincing. Dharmasvamin clearly suggests that Nalanda was in existence and nearly 70 monks lived there though Turkish raids were taking place. He himself stayed there and studied under Rahul Sribhadra.[24] Sumpa also tells us that Nalanda *Mahavihara* continued to exist even after the invasion of the Turks. Damaged and ruined *Viharas* were repaired or rebuilt and religious services were resumed by the Buddhists of Magadha after the Turkish invasion.[25] Still, the fact can not be denied that the Turkish raids caused immense damage to Nalanda *Mahavihara*.

Few lines may be added here regarding the motives of the Turkish invaders in attacking centres of education. It has been argued that "The military activities of the Turks were not marked by sacrilegious motives. The Turks were actuated by material considerations.... The writings of the Buddhist monks create the unhistorical impression that the Turkish soldiers were out on a mission of demolishing the Buddhistic religious and educational establishments and of reckless and inconsiderate killing of the people. Probably, the Turkish attack on the walled and fortified University town of Nalanda was motivated by its rich stores."[26] However, this argument is one sided. The religious motives behind the Turkish raids can not be altogether denied. Behind political and economic considerations religious aspect also played no less important role as is evidenced by the subsequent history of the Turks in India.

Religious Factors

Religious factors also played a major role in the decline of the *Mahaviharas*. This was on two counts, firstly, sectarian conflicts and secondly, inherent vices in *Mahayana* Buddhism, specially *Tantrayana, Mantrayana* and *Vajrayana*. Some of the practices of the *Tantrics* and other unhealthy developments contributed to the decline of Buddhism as well as of the *Viharas*. Several religious sects in Buddhism had emerged. *Hinayana* also had not completely lost its ground. Rivalries and conflicts between these sects as well as with the Brahamanical sects had emerged as a feature in Magadha and elsewhere.

There are several references to this conflict in contemporary Buddhist sources. The *Tirthikas* and the *Saindhavasravkas* were quite active at Nalanda, Vajrasana and Vikramshila. Lama Taranatha mentions at several places conflicts between the *Tirthikas* and the *Mahayanists* at Vajrasana and Nalanda. If we are to believe the Lama, the *Tirthikas* destroyed eighty-four religious institutions (probably *Viharas*) by throwing fire taken out of sacrificial pit (*yajnakunda*). In this fire the Dharmaganja consisting of Ratnasagar, Ratnodadhi and Ratnakarand, where all texts of the *Mahayana Pitaka* were preserved safely, were completely burnt.[27] He also refers to an incident which took place at Vajrasana. During the reign of king Dharmapala of Pala dynasty, the *Saindhavasravakas*, mostly the *bhikshus* of Simhala (Ceylon) created trouble at Vajrasana. They broke into pieces a silver made grand statue of Heruka kept in a *vihara* and burnt many books of *Mantrayana* kept there. They even incited the people coming from Bhangal (Bengal) against the *Mahayanists*.[28] This event took place when Vikramshila *Mahavihara* had been just established by Dharmapala. He punished these Simhalese monks. Though these instances are mentioned by Lama Taranatha to exhibit the superiority of *Mahayana*, nevertheless they suggest infighting and bickrings and secretarian rivalries amongst the Buddhists which ultimately caused the decline of Buddhism as well as Buddhist educational centres. Similar had the effect between the Buddhists and the Brahamanic *Mimamsakaras*. Fed up by secterian rivalries and annoyed with the *Tantric* practices some monks also might have taken side of the invading Turks. As Taranatha suggests, many of them even worked as agents of the advancing Turks.

More damaging, however, was the conduct of the *Tantrics*. The *Mahayana* form of Buddhism, assumed a darker and debased form of *Tantricism*. Magic, sorceries, secret rites, and rituals introduced into later Buddhism, particularly in respect of the female deities, alienated the common people. They did not come to the rescue of either the monks or their *Viharas*. When the final onslaught was made by the Turks on the *Viharas*, particularly Odantapuri and Vikramshila which were chief centres of *Tantricism*, anti-Buddhist forces kept themselves away, rather they helped them directly or indirectly in the destruction of the monasteries.

Socio-Economic Causes

Socio-economic factors also helped the decline of the *Mahaviharas*. The society in early medieval Bihar was sharply polarised. The feudal structure of the society created two distinct social groups–elite and commoners. While the first group indulged in luxurious living the commoners lived in abject poverty. This social inequality, coupled with caste rigidity, untouchability and other vices divided the society sharply. In such a situation the common people kept themselves aloof and did not come in support of the monks or monasteries. No institution could survive without the general support of the people. This became true in the case of the *Mahaviharas* of Bihar as well.

Coupled with social causes economic factors also contributed significantly in the decline of the Buddhist centres of education. These centres thrived on the financial support received from their patron kings, feudal chiefs, merchants and other devotees, but due to disturbed political situation their economic status declined and they became unable to support the monasteries. Their economic position itself faced crisis in face of emerging feudal economy marked by closed economy, decline of trade, towns and monetary economy in early medieval India.

In such a situation grants and endowments to *Viharas* decreased causing serious financial crisis for the *Mahaviharas*. It is surprising that except land grants made to Nalanda *Mahavihara* by Devapala and statements of Hsuan Tsang and I-Tsing that Nalanda was maintained by the revenue of 100 and 200 villages respectively, no such evidence of land grant in case of either Odantapuri or Vikramshila is available. We do not know exactly how these *Mahaviharas* were supported financially. Perhaps, endowments and donations were made to them in form of gold, silver and other precious metals. In due course of time these *Viharas* became repository of rich and valuable treasure. The richness of the *Mahaviharas* also became a cause of their decline. The Turks raided and looted wealth stored therein and in the process destroyed the *Mahaviharas*.

Thus, by the beginning of the 13th century CE except Nalanda, Odantapuri and Vikramshila *Mahaviharas* were completely destroyed. The political instability, Turkish raid, sectarian conflicts and rivalries, migration of scholars from the *Mahaviharas,* socio-economic degeneration made difficult for early medieval universities of India to survive and they were lost for ever in pages of history.

REFERENCES

1. George Roerich (trns.) *Biography of Dharmasvamin*, Patna, 1959.
2. Rigzin Lundup Lama (trns.), *Bharat Mein Baudha Dharma Ka Itihasa* (in Hindi), Patna, 1971.
3. Roerich, *op.cit.*, p. 64. For a detailed account of the political condition and condition of Buddhist educational centres at the time of Dharmasvamin's stay in India (1234-36 CE), see, *Ibid.*, pp. xviii-xxii, pp. 57-97.
4. Rigzin Lundup Lama, *op.cit.*, p. refers to several instances of Turkish raids and destruction of *Viharas*, pp. 53, 80-81, 124, 129, 134.
5. *J.A.S.B.*, LXVII (1898), p. 25. R.K. Chaudhary (*op.cit.*, p. 54) refers to a text the *Sambhala-Lam-Yig* which contains more or less similar account of the destruction of Universities by the Turks.

6. For details, see, H.G. Raverty (Eng. translation), *Tabqat-i-Nasiri*, p. 552.
7. A. Ghosh, *Nalanda (2006)*, p. 29. Evidence of fire was also noticed at Monastery Site No. 4 (p. 24).
8. Hiranand Sastri, *Nalanda And It's Epigraphical Material*, p. 107.
9. D.R. Patil, *The Antiquarian Remains in Bihar*, p. 325.
10. Rigzin Lundup Lama, *op.cit.*, pp. 55.
11. D.R. Patil, *op.cit.*, pp. 324-325.
12. *Ibid.*, p. 47.
13. A.K. Singh and Dilip Kumar, *Antichak Excavation Report (1960-69).*
14. *Ibid.*, p. 33.
15. *Ibid.*, p. 19.
16. B.S. Verma, *Antichak Excavations-2 (1971-1981)*, p. 10.
17. *Comprehensive History of Bihar*, Vol. II, Part I, p. 30. For a good account of the history of the Palas, see, B.P. Sinha, *Decline of the Kingdom of Magadha*, R.C. Majumdar (ed.) *History of Bengal*, Vol. I and *Comprehensive History of Bihar*, Vol. I, pt. II.
18. *Comprehensive History of Bihar*, Vol. II, Part I, pp. 30-31.
19. Rigzin Lundup Lama, *op.cit.*, p. 134.
20. For details see, S. Vidyabhushan, *History of Medieval Schools of Indian Logic*, pp. 151-152, 245. see also, Rigzin Lundup Lama, *op.cit.*, pp. 129, 134 ff.
21. *Comprehensive History of Bihar*, Vol. II, Pt. I, p. 33.
22. D.R. Patil, *op.cit.*, p. 304.
23. *Ibid.*, pp. 304, 324.
24. For details, see, George Roerich, *op.cit.*, pp. 90-97. See also, B.N. Mishra, *Nalanda*, Vol. I, pp. 211, 213 where he suggests that Nalanda probably survived at least upto the 15th century CE. In 16th century Nalanda came to be known as Badgama, later Baragaon.
25. *JASB*, ixvii, p. 26, *Glories of Magadha*, pp. 102, 134.
26. *Comprehensive History of Bihar*, Vol. II, Pt. I, p. 40. Some scholars have questioned the role of Turkish invaders in the destruction of the *Mahaviharas* and argue that it is based on nationalist

assumption. They also question the account of the Tibetans. To quote them, "The writings of the Buddhist monks create the unhistorical impression that the Turkish soldiers were out on mission of demolishing the Buddhist religious and educational establishments and of reckless and inconsiderable killing of the people. In fact, the Turks had no well thought out plan, decided in advance, to demolish or ruin utterly the Buddhist monastery and killing the people." See, K. K. Mandal and Asha Kumari, "The Destruction of Vikramshila Mahavihara - A Revist" in R. K. Sinha and O.P. Pandey (ed), *op.cit.*, pp. 222-234, However, such statements are merely denying historical facts.

27. Rigzin Lundup Lama, *op.cit.*, p. 55. See pp. 73 and 91 also where dispute among the *Mahayanists* and the *Tirthikas* is mentioned and how Santideva became victorious over the *Tirthikas*. Taranatha also informs us that during the rule of the Senas the influence of the *Tirthikas* and *Mlechchas* (Turks) increased considerably in Magadha (p. 133).

28. *Ibid.*, p. 118.

7

Epilogue

Early medieval India made significant contribution in the field of education. Two distinct systems of education developed here – the Brahamanical and the Buddhist. The Brahamanical educational system evolved around the hermitages of *Rsis* and *Gurukulas* while the Buddhist one around the *Viharas* and *Samgharamas*. The *gurukula* mode of education could not survive for long but the monastic system of education became more widespread and popular with the passage of time. Whereas no *gurukula* could develop into a centre of higher education, several *viharas* evolved as organised centres of higher education and came to be known as the *Mahaviharas* or 'Universities'. Surprisingly, the contribution of the Jains in the development of education in early medieval Bihar was almost negligible. We are yet to come across any full-fledged Jain educational institution in early medieval Bihar.

The Brahamanical system of education was older than the monastic system. Its origin can be traced back to the *Vedic* period itself but it gained ground in the *Upanishadic* period and subsequent centuries. Even after the establishment of regular educational centres in medieval and modern times, it continued to flourish in some form or other in temples, *mathas*, and *agraharas*, especially in South India. The main centre of Brahamincal education in early medieval Bihar was Mithila. The monastic system of education developed with the emergence of Buddhism and the *Viharas* and continued upto the beginning of the 13th century CE. Both the systems laid stress on the development of knowledge and personality, infusion of spirit of piety and religiousness, inculcation of civil, social and moral duties. Religion formed an important subject of study, though language, literature, logic, philosophy, scientific knowledge and other secular subjects were not neglected. Whereas *Upanayan* ceremony formed the main ritual of the Brahamnical system of education, *Pabbajja* or *Pravrajya*, similar to *Upanayana*, was initiation ceremony for the Buddhist students.

With the spread of Buddhism *Viharas* came to be set up for residence of the monks which also served as schools for teaching of the monks. In Bihar large number of *Viharas* came to be set up mostly in the then Vrijji land (Vaishali) and Magadha. Some of them like Vajrasana (Bodh Gaya), Rajgir, Nalanda, Ghosrawan, Telhara, Odantapuri, Pataliputra in South Bihar, Champa and Antichak (Bhagalpur) in North Bihar, developed as major centres of Buddhist studies. Of these Nalanda, Odantapuri and Vikramshila acquired the status of *Mahaviharas* (Universities). Information about the teaching and studies at these *Mahaviharas* and their working is derived mainly from the Chinese and Tibetan literary sources. The archaeological excavations carried out at some of these sites, exposed architectural remains, bronze images, stone sculptures, terracotta plaques, seals-sealings and inscriptions throwing abundant light on these *Viharas*.

The Mahabodhi *Samgharama* and Vajrasana was situated at Bodh Gaya, one of the most sacred places for the Buddhists. Fa-hien informs us that the teaching of *Vinaya* rules was imparted there. By the time of the visit of Hsuan Tsang, the Mahabodhi *Samgharama* had developed as an important centre of Buddhist education. This *Samgharama* was built by king Meghavarna of Ceylon for the convenience of the Ceylonese monks. At the time of Hsuan Tsang's visit more than 1000 priests or monks lived there and studied the *Great Vehicle*. The construction of the Ceylonese monastery is confirmed by the inscription of Mahanaman, a resident of Amradvipa born in Sri Lanka. The remains of this *Samgharama* were located by Cunningham at Amar Singh's Fort, north of the Mahabodhi Temple.

Rajagir, also known as Rajagriha, Vasumati, Brahadrathapura, Kusagrapura, Magadhapura, Girivraja, Bimbisarapura, was the capital of the Magadhan empire before it was transferred to Pataliputra. The place finds repeated mention in the Brahamanic, Buddhist and Jain literature as well as in the travelogues of the Chinese pilgrims. Both Fa-hien and Hsuan Tsang refer to several *Viharas*, at Rajagriha the most important being the Jivakarama *Vihara*, but they do not tell us about the system of education prevailing there. Probably these monasteries had lost their importance after the transfer of capital from Rajagriha to Pataliputra, though some monks might have lived there.

Nalanda, close to Rajgir, identified with village Baragaon and adjoining villages, has the distinction of being the first full-fledged Buddhist University. Long years of excavations have exposed the remains of the monastic complex. Detailed account of this University is preserved in the writings of Husan Tsang and I-Tsing. Several seals, sealings and inscriptions, enlightening us on the history of this monastic educational centre are available.

Ghosrawan near Biharsharif, named as Yasovarmanpura after king Yasovarman of Kanauj, seems to be an important centre of Buddhist studies. It had acquired considerable fame so that a scholar named Viradeva of Nagrahara (Afghanistan), having completed his studies at Peshawar (Kanishka *Vihara*), came to study at Yasovarmanpura and was later on appointed as chief abbot of Nalanda *Mahavihara*.

Telhara in Ekangarasarai *grama panchayat* of present Nalanda district, appears to be an important educational centre. Hsuan Tsang describes in detail the construction of this monastery and says that there were nearly 1000 priests who studied *Great Vehicle*. Prajnabhadra of Telhara (Tiladaka) had earned fame as a scholar and Hsuan Tsang met him. The Directorate of Archaeology, Government of Bihar, took up exacavation work at the site between 2009 and 2014. Apart from other antiquities, several terracotta seals have been discovered during excavations.

On the basis of a seal discovered from the site recently it has been claimed that the real name of Telhara was *'Sri Prathamashipur University'* *(Sri Prathamashivpur Mahavihariyaye Bhikshu Sanghas)*. It has been also claimed that this university was older than Nalanda. This seems questionable. Only further excavations may throw light on Telhara.

Odantapuri at Biharsharif was established by king Gopala, founder of the Pala dynasty. It became a renowned University and centre of *Tantric* studies. No systematic and extensive excavation of the site could be made but the Tibetan sources inform us about this University.

Pataliputra (modern Patna) was another important educational centre, Brahamnical as well as Buddhist. Both Fa-hien and Hsuan Tsang visited this place. Probably, Pataliputra gained educational importance after the decline of Taxila (Takshshila), the ancient seat of Vedic learning and 'intellectual capital of India'. It was only in Pataliputra that Fa-hien could procure a copy of manuscript of *Vinaya* not available elsewhere in India. Pataliputra remained as an important educational centre upto 4-5th centuries of the Christian era, but it lost its importance by the time Hsuan Tsang came to this city.

Vaishali, was a renowned monastic centre with a number of *Viharas* dating from the days of Gautam Buddha, the most important being the Kutagarasala. As the Second Buddhist Council was held in Vaishali it is suggestive of the fact that the ancient city remained an important centre of Buddhist studies, at least in the pre-Gupta period. Several *Viharas* were noticed by Fa-hien and Hsuan Tsang in Champa, also, the capital of ancient Anga. However, details about them are not known. Mention may be made here about Kukutapadagiri *Vihara* or Apanaka *Mahavihara*. The place has been identified with Kurkihar near Wazirganj in Gaya district, famous for its bronze images. Remains of a *stupa* and several monastic cells were exposed here. Some of the bronze images were inscribed in which names of Pala kings Devapala, Rajapala (Rajyapala), Mahipala I and Vigrahapala III appear. Phullhari, also known as Pushpahari, seems to be an important centre of Buddhist education. Naropa, the famous *Tantric Siddha* and scholar lived in this monastery for nearly six years and then moved on to Vikramshila. The location of this University is a matter of controversy. R.K. Chaudhary was inclined to locate it near Naulagarh in Begusarai district while others locate it somewhere near Nalanda in Magadha. The later view is now generally accepted. Apart from Naropa, several other scholars lived here and translated several Sanskrit texts into the Tibetan language.

In the Anga region most important educational centre was Vikramshila *Mahavihara,* identified with village Antichak near Kahalgaon in Bhagalpur. It was established by king Dharmapala of the Pala dynasty. It was the chief centre of *Tantric* studies.

Recently excavations conducted in Krimila region in Lakhsarai atop Lalpahari in Jayanagar has brought to light remains of yet another *Vihara* known as Srimaddharma *vihara.* Two burnt inscribed sealings were found from here. The inscription read as *Srimaddharmaviharika aryabhiksusanghasya* ('This is the sealing) of the council of monks of Srimaddhamavihara (monastery'). This sanskrit inscription belongs to 8/9 century CE. The name of the *vihara* suggests a close connection with *Mahayana* esoteric practices. However, details about the *vihara* is yet to come out.

All these educational centres went out of existence by the beginning of the 13th century CE, due to combination of several factors. Points of similarity and differences between Brahamanical and Buddhist system of education have been noticed. The main difference between the two was that whereas the Brahamanical system was depended entirely on the capability of individual teacher, the Buddhist system revolved around *Viharas* and was well organised. No brahamanical educational centre, not even Mithila, could emerge as organised University like Nalanda, Odantapuri and Vikramshila and acquire national and international reputation.

The oldest full-fledged University of early medieval India was Nalanda *Mahavihara*. The ruins of Nalanda have been identified with Baragaon in Nalanda district and several adjoining villages lying at a distance of nearly 7 miles north of Rajgir and at equal distance south-west of Biharsharif, the district headquarters of Nalanda. The site was first brought to notice by Francis Buchanan in 1811-12. It was, however, Alexander Cunningham, who convincingly, on the basis of two inscriptions discovered from Baragaon, suggested that the site actually represents the ruins of Nalanda *Mahavihara*. Since then several excavations were conducted at the site by the Archaeological Survey of India, the latest being the excavations conducted by Birendra Nath at Sarai Mound (1978-82). These excavations have exposed remains of a huge monastic complex and nearly 690 seals and sealings referring to different royal persons, *viharas*, villages, administrative units, etc. Several inscriptions were also discovered from here which are very important for the study of the history of Nalanda. We are also indebted to the Chinese pilgrims Hsuan Tsang and I-Tsing for giving us a detailed account of this University. To some extent, Lama Taranatha's *History of Buddhism in India* and Dharmasvamin's account of Nalanda, also help us considerably in this effort, specially regarding the later part of the history of this world famous University.

Different traditions exist regarding the etymology of Nalanda. Before the establishment of the *Mahavihara*, Nalanda was an important religious centre where followers of different sects more than often met, including the Buddhists. It was at this place that king Sakaraditya (Kumaragupta I of Gupta dynasty) laid the foundations of the *Vihara* in or about 425 CE. Ever since its establishment the monastery received patronage of other Gupta kings namely Skandagupta, Purugupta, Narasimhagupta and Kumaragupta II. They built new monasteries at Nalanda. Later on the Maukharis, Harshavardhan of Kanauj and Palas of Bengal and Bihar extended their support and patronage to this *Mahavihara*. It was during the reign of Devapala that king Balaputradeva of Suvarnadvipa built a monastery at Nalanda and on his request Devapala made a grant of five villages for the maintenance of this monastery. Nalanda fell on bad days, after the weakening of the Pala authority over Bịhar. The invasion of Bakhtiyar Khalji around 1203 CE gave it a shattering blow though it survived some how. Dharmasvamin, the Tibetan monk's (1234-36 CE) account suggests that Nalanda existed as a mere ghost of its past glory during his stay.

In its heydays Nalanda *Mahavihara* was a huge monastic complex, consisting of several *Viharas* with lofty towers and pinnacles, with gardens and lotus ponds and supported by the revenue received from 100 (Hsuan Tsang) and 200 (I-Tsing) villages. The archaeological excavations have brought to light remains of nearly eleven monasteries *(Viharas)* with provision of cells for monks and several Temples *(Chaityas?)*, the most important one being the Temple site No. 3.

Nalanda's fame rests primarily on its educational system where students and knowledge seekers not only from different corners of India but distant places like China and South-East Asia congregated in good number. An unique feature of this University was that the admission seekers in the University had to pass oral test conducted by the *Dwarapandits*, who were themselves eminent scholars. The students were put under strict discipline though parental relationship existed between the teacher and taught. The teaching method put more stress on memorisation of sacred texts, debates and discussions than on class room lectures. The *Mahavihara* enjoyed complete autonomy in its administration and issued its own seal. It was run on democratic pattern, different committees of monks under the control of the chief abbot managed the affairs of the University. The curriculum of the University was very vast. It covered not only theology but language, literature, logic, philosophy, *Tantra*, medicine, astronomy, art and iconography but even copying of manuscripts of sacred texts. Theology seems to be compulsory subject. Great stress was put on the study of *Mahayana* Buddhism. It appears from Lama Taranatha's account that Nalanda University possessed vast collection of manuscripts preserved in its library *(Dharmaganja)* though remains of this library were not exposed during excavations at Nalanda. Many eminent scholars like Asanga, Vasubandhu, Dinnaga, Sthirmati,

Gunamati, Dharmapala, Silabhadra, Nagarjuna, Santideva, Santarakshita, Padmasambha, Viradeva and Dipankarasrijnan Atisa contributed to the eminence of this University. Scholars from China, Tibet, Korea, Tukhara country and other places came to Nalanda, resided there and gained knowledge. Similarly, scholars from Nalanda went to foreign land and spread the tennents of *Mahayana* Buddhism, specially *Tantrayana* and *Vajrayana*. Nalanda also maintained close relations with other contemporary Buddhist centres of learning like Vallabhi, Vajrasana, Odantapuri, Vikramshila, Somapura and Jagaddal. Thus, Nalanda became an international University.

Close to Nalanda was also established the *Mahavihara* of Odantapuri or "flying city" in 8th century CE. It was situated in the modern town of Biharsharif, the district headquarters of Nalanda district. The *Mahavihara* is believed to have been established by Gopala, the founder of the Pala dynasty. Details about this *Mahavihara* are not available due to limited excavations and explorations at Biharsharif. Odantapuri was famous for *Tantric* studies. The eminent scholars connected with this University were Santarakshita, Silarakshita, Dipamkarasrijnan Atisa and two *Siddhas* Yoga pa and Snati-pa. It was Santarakshita who got constructed Sam-ye *Vihara* in Tibet on the model of Odantapuri *Mahavihara* and introduced Buddhist monasticism there. The scholars of Odantapuri maintained close contact with Nalanda and Vikramshila as well as Tibet. The *Mahavihara* was completely destroyed by Bakhtiyar Khalji towards the close of 12th century CE.

Information about Vikramshila *Mahavihara* is preserved mainly in the Tibetan accounts. The exact location of this *Mahavihara* was a matter of controversy for long time but the excavations carried out at village Antichak near Kahalgaon in Bhagalpur district by the Department of Ancient Indian History and Archaeology, Patna University and the Archaeological Survey of India, have more or less confirmed that the *Mahavihara* was situated at Antichak. However, conclusive evidence in the form of seal or inscription mentioning the name of Vikramshila is yet to be discovered. Perhaps it was known to the people as

Rajayagrara (ha) Mahavihara or *rajjaya vihara* as found inscribed on two seals discovered from Antichak. The excavations have brought to light remains of several structures, including a huge monastic complex and massive *stupa*.

Vikramshila *Mahavihara* was established by the Pala king Dharmapala. It was more or less a royal University and did not enjoy internal autonomy like Nalanda. The Pala kings accorded their patronage to this University. It was main centre of *Tantric* studies in India. *Tnatrayana* and *Vajrayana* formed the main subjects of study, though other branches were not altogether neglected. There were six *Dwarapandits* to examine the eligibility of the students and scholars before admitting them to the University. The *Mahavihara* conducted some kind of convocation at the completion of studies and degrees or diplomas of *Pandit* were conferred on successful candidates by the reigning Pala king. The University put great stress on inculcating strong moral character *(Shila)*. It was perhaps one of the reasons why this University was also named as Vikramshila. the University maintained close contact with other sister Universities and Tibet. Large number of Tibetans resided and studied at Vikramshila. Eminent scholars and some of the 84 *Siddhas* were related with this *Mahavihara* in one way or another. Mention may be made of Buddhajnanpada, Ratnakarsanti, Prajnakaramati, Vagiswarkirti, Naropa, Dipamkarasrijnana Atisa, Jetari, Abhayankaragupta and Sakayasribhadra, the last chief abbot of Vikramshila. It was during his times that the fear of Turkish invasion increased considerably. He, therefore, with large number of monks left the *Mahavihara* and went to Tibet. While passing through Bhagalpur on way to Bengal, Bakhtiyar Khalji destroyed violently Vikramshila *Mahavihara* as he had done earlier at Odantapuri. The destruction was so disastrous and complete that the *Mahavihara* could never revive there after.

Except Nalanda *Mahavihara*, all other major *Mahaviharas* of Bihar survived for nearly four centuries between 8th and 12th centuries. They contributed immensely to the advancement of knowledge, specially *Mahayana* Buddhism with its different facades. By the beginning of 13th century they all went out of existence. Nalanda survived for some more time but Odantapuri and Vikramshila completely lost their identity. Even before their final destruction, there is archaeological evidence from Nalanda, and Vikramshila to suggest that the monasteries suffered damage on account of fire and some kind of violent activities causing damage to the structures. Therefore, they were rebuilt, but could not survive for long. The Tibetan sources suggest that the final destruction was caused by the Turkish raids of Bakhtiyar Khalji. However, it must be admitted that the Turkish raids were only one of the causes of the destruction of the *Mahaviharas*. Several other factors combined together to bring about the decline and disappearance of the *Mahaviharas*. The weakening of the Pala authority over Bihar and Bengal and following political instability and chaos made the peaceful existence of these *Mahaviharas* somewhat impossible. Monks and scholars left Nalanda, Odantapuri, Vikramshila and other *Viharas*, migrated to safer places, specially Tibet. The political unrest also snapped the financial support base of the *Mahaviharas*. Religious factors also played a significant role in the decline of the *Mahaviharas*. The sectarian conflicts and rivalries as well as inherent vices in *Mahayana* Buddhism, particularly *Tantrayana*, *Mantrayana* and *Vajrayana* and the conduct of the *Tantrics*, alienated the people. The *Viharas* lost sympathy and support of the masses. When the Turks raided and plundered them, none came to defend them. Moreover, the emerging scoio-economic feudal structure also caused decline of the *Mahaviharas* of India. The shattering blow was, of course, given by the Turks.

Bibliography

Altekar, A.S. and Vijayakant Mishra, *Kumhrar Excavations (1951-56)*, Patna, 1959.

– –, *Education in Ancient India*, Varanasi, 1957 (5th edition).

Apte, D.G., *Universities in Ancient India.*

Archaeological Survey of India Reports, (Relevant Volumes).

Arun Kumar, "The Concept of Education in Early India (From Vedic period up to 600 A.D)" in C.P. Sinha (ed.) *Art, Archaeology and Cultural History of India,* New Delhi.

Askari, S.H. and Q. Ahmad (ed.), *The Comprehensive History of Bihar,* Vol. II, Pt. I, Patna, 1983.

Barua, D.K., *Viharas in Ancient India,* Calcutta, 1969.

– –, *Gaya and Buddha Gaya,* 2 vols., 1934.

Beal, S. (trns.), *Buddhist Records of the Western World,* 2 vols, Delhi, 2003 (Reprint)

– –, *The Life of Hiuen Tsang by Shaman Hwui-Li,* Delhi, 1973 (Reprint).

Bose, P.N., *The Indian Teachers in China,* Madras, 1923.

– –, *Eminent Teachers of Buddhist Universities,* Madras, 1923.

Buchanan, H, *Patna-Gaya.*

Buston, *A History of Buddhism,* E. Obermiller (trns.), 2 parts, Heidelberg, 1931-32.

Chattopadhyaya, Alka, *Atisa and Tibet: Life and Works of Dipankara Srijnana in relation to the history and religon of Tibet,* Calcutta, 1967.

– –, *Mahabodhi.*

Chaudhary, B.K., "Identifying the surroundings of Nalanda Mahavihara", *Purattatva*, no. 38, 2008, pp. 91-101.

Chaudhary, Binayendranath, *Buddhist Centres in Ancient India*, Calcutta, 1969.

Chaudhary, R.K., *Bihar the Homeland of Buddhism*, Patna, 1956.

– –, *Inscriptions of Bihar*.

– –, *History of Bihar*, Varanasi, 1958.

– –, *The University of Vikramshila*, The Bihar Research Society, Patna, 1975.

Chimpa, Lama and Alka Chattopadhyaya (trns.), *Taranath's History of Buddhism in India*, Shimla, 1970.

Cunningham, Alexander, *Ancient Geography of India*, Varanasi, 1975 (Reprint).

– –, *Archaeological Survey of India Reports*, 1861.

Das, S.C., *Indian Pandits in the Land of Snow*, Calcutta, 1965 (2nd edn).

Das, S.K., *The Education System of the Ancient Hindus*, Delhi, 1986 (Reprint).

Datta, Sukumar, *Buddhist Monks and Monasteries of India*, 1962.

Davids, Rhys (ed.), *Digha Nikaya*, PTS, London, 1890-1911.

Diwakar, R.R., *Bihar Through the Ages*, Patna, 2001 (Reprint).

Dwivedi, Shyamdeo, "Ancient University of Nalanda and Its Famous Teachers", *Nalanda Mahavihara Research*, Vol. III, pp. 1-11.

Ghosh, A., *Nalanda*, Archaeological Survey of India, New Delhi, 2006 (7th ed.).

Indian Archaeology – A Review, Archaeological Survey of India, New Delhi (1953 onwards).

Jacobi, H. (trns.), *Jain Sutras, SBE*, Vol. XLV.

Jha, Jatashankar, *Education in Bihar*, Patna, 1979.

Jha, Satyendra Kumar, *Rajagrha: The City of Eminence*, K.P. Jayaswal Research Institute, Patna, 2011.

Kameshwar Prasad, "Pataliputra : Arambh se 1912 Tak", pp. 53-80 in *Sau Saal mein Patna*, Bihar Vidhan Parishad, Patna, 1912.

– –,*The Glory that was Vaishali*, Patna, 2015.

Keay, F.E., *Ancient Indian Education*, Delhi, 1980 (Reprint).

Krishna Deva and Vijayakant Mishra, *Vaishali Excavations, 1950,* Vaishali Sangh, 1861.

Kumar, N., *Patna District Gazetteer,* Govt. of Bihar, 1970.

Kuraishi, M.A., *A Short Guide to the Buddhist Remains,* Calcutta, 1931.

– –, *List of Ancient Monuments.*

Lal, B.B., *Nalanda,* Patna, 1953.

Law, B.C., *Early Indian Monasteries,* Bangalore, 1958.

– –, *Historical Geography of Ancient India.*

Legge, James, *A Record of Buddhistic Kingdoms,* Delhi, 1993 (Reprint).

Majumdar, N.M., *A History of Education in Ancient India,* Calcutta, 1916.

Majumdar, R.C. (ed.), *History of Bengal,* Vol. I, Delhi 2003 (Reprint).

Maxmuller (ed.), *Jain Sutras, SBE,* Vol. XXII.

Mishra, B.N., *Nalanda,* 3 vols., Delhi, 2008.

Mishra, Jayadeo, *Rise and Fall of Universities in Ancient Bihar,* Patna, 1980.

Mishra, Shiva Kumar, *Educational Ideas and Institutions,* New Delhi, 1998.

Mishra, Yogendra, "University of Odantapuri", *The Journal of the Bihar, History Congress,* Patna, No. 1, 2008, pp. 25-44.

– –, *An Early History of Vaishali,* Motilal Banarsidas, 1962.

– –, *Homage to Vaishali,* 1985.

Mitra, Debala, *Buddhist Monuments,* Calcutta, 1971.

Mookerji, R.K., *Ancient Indian Education* (Brahmanical and Buddhist), Motilal Banarsidas, 1960 (3rd edition).

Nath, B., *Nalanda Murals,* 1983.

Pandey, M.S., *Historical Geography and Topography of Bihar,* Delhi, 1963.

Panth, R (ed.), *Nalanda and Buddhism and the World,* Nava Nalanda Mahavihara, Nalanda, 2001.

– –, *Nalanda and Buddhism,* Nava Nalanda Mahavihara, Nalanda, 2002.

Patil, D.R., *The Antiquarian Remains in Bihar,* Patna, 1963.

Prasad, Birendra Nath (ed.), *Monasteries, Shrines and Sociaty: Buddhist and Brahmanical Religions Instituions in India in their Socio-Economic Context,* New Delhi, 2011.

Prasad, Birendra Nath (ed.), "The social Bases of Patronage to the Vikramshila Mahavihara: An Epigraphic Enquiry", in Rajiv Kumar Sinha and Om Prakash Pandey (ed), *op.cit.*, pp. 49-64.

Prasad, R.C., *Archaeology of Champa and Vikramshila*, Delhi, 1987.

Rigzin Lundup Lama, *Bharat Mein Bauddha Dharm ka Itihasa* (in Hindi), Patna, 1971.

Roerich, G. (trns.), *Biography of Dharmasvamin*, K.P. Jayaswal Research Institute, Patna, 1959.

Roth, Gustav, *Arama, Vihara and Mahavihara*, Patna, 1997.

Roychaudhary, P. C., *Bihar District Gazetters*, Patna, 1962.

Roychaudhuri, H.C., *Political History of Ancient India*, Oxford, 2006 (Seventh impression).

Sahai, Bhagwant, *The Inscriptions of Bihar*, Delhi, 1983.

Sahaya, Kiran, *Vikramshila; Itihasa Evam Puratattva* (in Hindi), Patna, 1998.

Samadar, J.N., *The Glories of Magadha*, Patna, 1990 (3rd edn.).

Sankalia, H.D., *The University of Nalanda*, Oriental Publication, Delhi, 1972 (2nd Revised and enlarged edn.).

Sankrityana, Rahul, *Puratattva Nibandhawali* (in Hindi), Prayaga, 1937.

– –, *Tibet Mein Bauddha Dharma* (in Hindi).

Sarkar, S.C., *Educational Ideas and Institutions in Ancient India*, Janaki Prakashan, Patna, 1979.

Sastri, Hiranand, *Nalanda and Its Epigraphical Materials, MASI*, No. 66, Delhi, 1986 (Reprint).

Sen, A.C., *Rajagriha and Nalanda*, Calcutta, 1964.

– – (ed), *Buddhist Remains in India*, New Delhi, 1956.

Singh, A.K. and Dilip Kumar, *Antichak Excavations (1960-69)*, Department of Ancient Indian History and Archaeology, Patna University.

Singh, Lal Babu, *Vikaramshila* (in Hindi), Sahitya Kunj, 1997, Patna.

Singh, Nirupama, "Nalanda and Vikramshila University: A Comparative Study", *Vikramshila Journal of Social Sciences*, Vol. 10, No. 2 (July-Dec. 2013).

Singh, Raman Kumar, *Palkalin Vikramshila Mahavihara*, Delhi, 2005.

Sinha, B.P. and L.A. Narain, *Pataliputra Excavations (1955-56)*, Patna, 1970.

Sinha, B.P. and Sita Ram Roy, *Vaishali Excavations (1958-62)*, Patna, 1969.

Sinha, B.P., *Directory of Bihar Archaeology*, Bihar Puravid Parisad, Patna, 2000.

– –, *The Decline of the Kingdom of Magadhah.*

Sinha, Rajiv Kumar, "The Making of Vikramshila Mahavihara: Material Milieu and Socio-religious context (CE 783-CE 1150)" in Rajiv Kumar Sinha and Om Prakash Pandey (ed.) *op.cit.*, pp. 34-48.

Sinha, Rajiv Kumar, Omprakash Pandey (ed.), *Studies in History and Archaeology of Vikramshila Mahavihara : The Last Beacon of Buddhist Philosophy*, Varanasi, 2015.

Sinha, S.P., 'Nalanda and Vikramshila', *Nava Nalanda Research*, Volume (no. VIII), pp. 281-291.

Sinha, Sujata, *Magadha, Early Education System*, B.R. Publishing Corporation, Delhi, 2014.

Sumpa, *Pag-sam-jon-zang* (ed.), S.C. Das, Calcutta, 1908.

Takakusu, J. (trns.), *A Record of the Buddhist Religion As Practised in India and the Malay Archipelago (AD 671-695)*, Delhi, 1966 (Reprint).

Thapalyal, K.K., *Studies in Ancient Indian Seals*, Lucknow, 1972.

Tripathi, Havaldar, *Buddha Dharam Aur Bihar*, Patna, 1960.

Upasaka, C.S. (ed.), *Nalanda Past and Present (Silver Jubilee Souvenir)*, Nava Nalanda Mahavihar, Nalanda, 1977.

Verma, B.S., *Antichak Excavation–2 (1971-1981)*, Archaeological Survey of India, New Delhi, 2011.

Vidyabhushan, S.C., *History of Indian Logic*, Calcutta, 1921.

Waddell, A., *Report on the Excavations at Pataliputra*, Delhi 1975 (Reprint).

Watters, T., *On Yuwan Chwang's Travels in India*, Delhi, 1961 (Reprint).

Index

D

E

F

G

H

I

J

K

L

M

PLATES

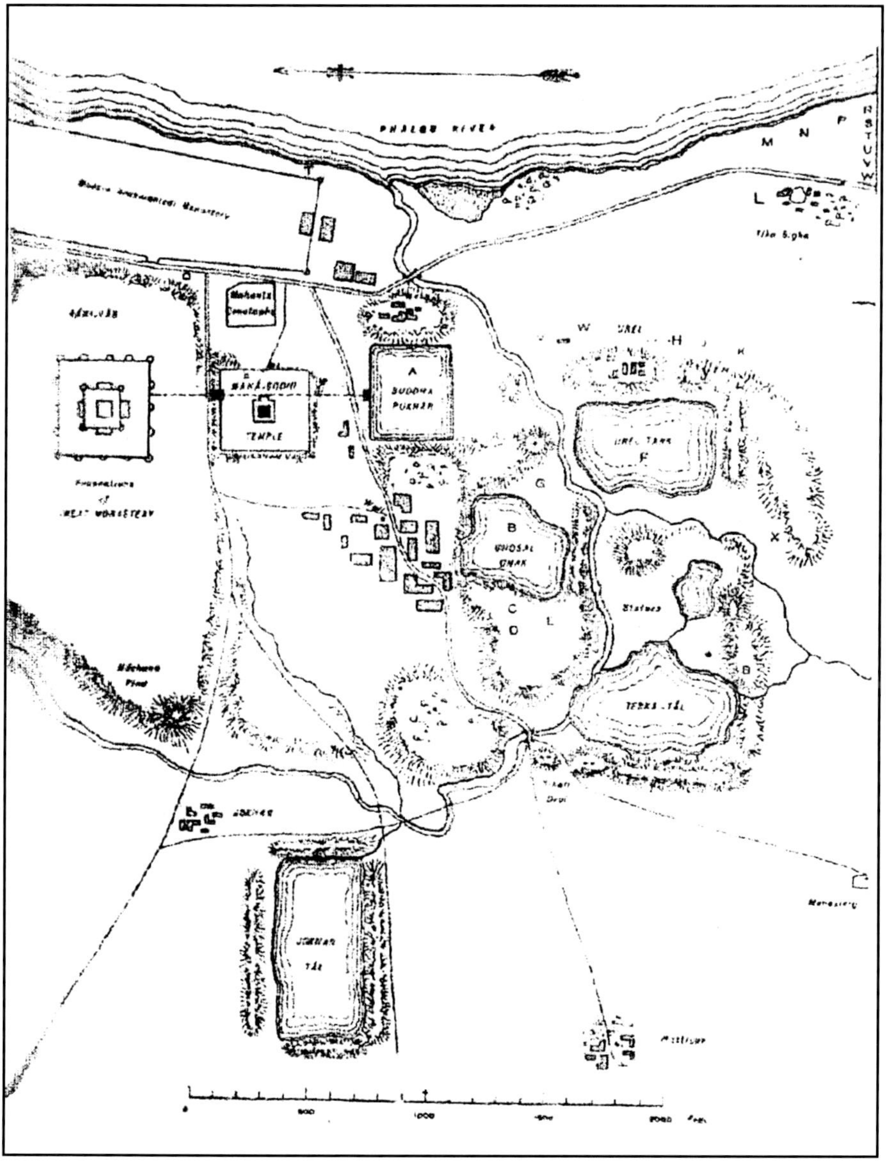

Plate 1: Foundation of the Mahabodhi Samgharama

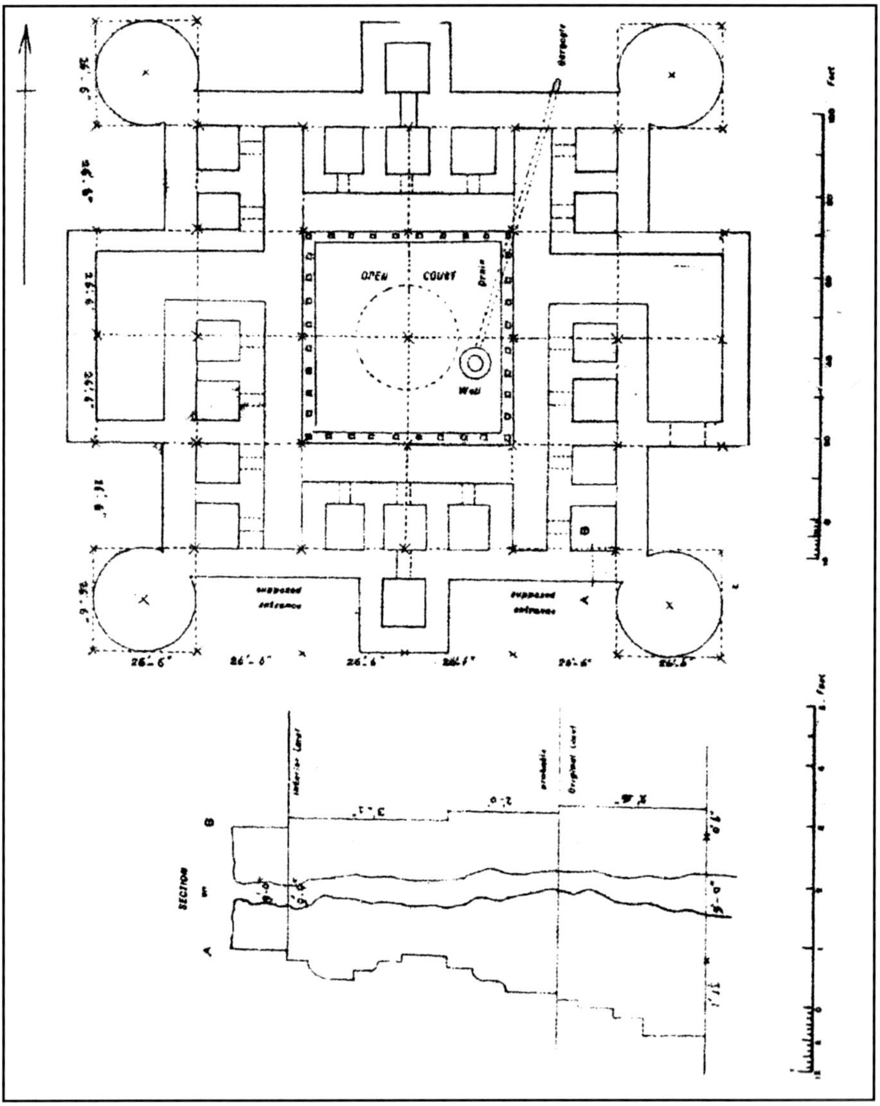

Plate 2: Plan of the Mahabodhi Samgharama

Plate 3: Jivakarama Viahara, Rajgir

Plate 4: An Overview of Telhara Excavations

Plate 5: Excavation in progress at Telhara

Plate 6: Monastic Complex, Telhara

Plate 7: Structural remains, Telhara

Plate 8: Exposed Structures, Telhara

Plate 9: Remains of Svastika Vihara, Kolhua, Vaishali

Plate 10: Seal of Nalanda Mahavihara

Plate 11: Samgharama built by Narasimhagpta, Baladitya, Nalanda

Plate 12: Monastic Complex, Nalanda

Plate 13: Temple No. 3, Nalanda

Plate 14: Corner tower and plinth of Temple no. 3, Nalanda

Plate 15: Remains of Sarai Mound Temple, Nalanda

Plate 16: Remains of the wall of the fort of Oddanda (Odantapuri) Mahavihara

Plate 17: Probable site of Odantapuri Mahavihara, Bari Pahadi, Biharsharif

Plate 18: Samaye Vihara, Tibet

Plate 19: Central shrine of Vikramshila Mahavihara

Plate 20: Another view of Central shrine, Vikramshila Mahavihara

Plate 21: Pathway connecting Central shrine with the main gate of Vikramshila Mahavihara

Plate 22: Remains of monastic complex, Vikramshila Mahavihara

Plate 23: Remains of Library Hall of Vikramshila Mahavihara